INQUIRY INTO CRUCIAL AMERICAN PROBLEMS

Series Editor · JACK R. FRAENKEL

Cities in Crisis:

Decay or Renewal?

RUDIE W. TRETTEN

Vice Principal for Guidance
Jefferson High School
Daly City, California

PRENTICE-HALL, INC.   ENGLEWOOD CLIFFS, N.J.

38332

Titles in this series:

Printed in the United States of America

ISBN 0-13-134684-9 paper
ISBN 0-13-134718-7 cloth

1 2 3 4 5 6 7 8 9 10

Prentice-Hall International, Inc.,
London
Prentice-Hall of Australia, Pty. Ltd.,
Sydney
Prentice-Hall of Canada, Ltd.,
Toronto
Prentice-Hall of India Private Ltd.,
New Delhi
Prentice-Hall of Japan, Inc.,
Tokyo

PREFACE

The series *INQUIRY INTO CRUCIAL AMERICAN PROB-LEMS* focuses upon a number of important contemporary social and political issues. Each book presents an in-depth study of a particular problem, selected because of its pressing intrusion into the minds and consciences of most Americans today. A major concern has been the desire to make the materials relevant to students. Every title in the series, therefore, has been selected because, in one way or another, it suggests a problem of concern to students today.

A number of divergent viewpoints, from a wide variety of different *kinds* of sources, encourage discussion and reflection and illustrate that the same problem may be viewed from many different vantage points. Of concern throughout is a desire to help students realize that honest men may legitimately differ in their views.

After a short chapter introducing the questions with which the book will deal, Chapter 2 presents a brief historical and contemporary background so that students will have more than just a superficial understanding of the problem under study. In the readings that follow, a conscientious effort has been made to avoid endorsing any one viewpoint as the "right" viewpoint, or to evaluate the arguments of particular individuals. No conclusions are drawn. Instead, a number of questions for discussion and reflection are posed at the end of each reading so that students can come to their own conclusions.

Great care has been taken to insure that the readings included in each book are just that—readable! We have searched particularly for articles that are of high interest, yet from which differing viewpoints may be legitimately inferred. Whenever possible, dialogues involving or descriptions showing actual people responding and reacting to problematic situations are presented. In sum, each book

- presents divergent, conflicting views on the problem under consideration;

- gives as many perspectives and dimensions on the problem as space permits;

- presents articles on a variety of reading levels, in order to appeal to students of many different ability levels;

- presents analytical as well as descriptive statements;

- deals with real people involved in situations of concern to them;

- includes questions which encourage discussion and thought of the various viewpoints expressed;

- includes activities to involve students to consider further the issues embedded in the problem.

CONTENTS

1

Introduction

The United States has become a nation of cities. For hundreds of years the trend toward an ever-greater concentration of people in cities has continued. Now over 70 per cent of the United States population lives in urban areas. Predictions are that this figure will rise to more than 80 per cent by 1980. Since our population increases by over two million people per year, this means that over 184 million Americans will be living within the boundaries of an urban area at that time.

Why do people live in cities? Presumably they live in them because life is better there than elsewhere. Cities mean jobs; cities are centers of man's great cultural achievements; cities have great universities; cities offer excitement and action. In short, the city attracts people for many reasons and holds them for just as many reasons. Essentially, however, the city is the promise of something better. The great problem with cities is that often the promise is not fulfilled.

American cities are in trouble. There are many reasons for this. Cities have been successful in attracting and keeping people, but the central sections of cities are growing older and have become racial and social class ghettos. The automobile is taking an increasing percentage of city land for freeways and parking spaces. High-rise buildings create greater and greater densities of people living and working together. Human greed and prejudice allow some humans to live well at the expense of others, who must live in degraded circumstances. But perhaps the greatest problem facing our cities is our refusal as a nation to make the kinds of adjustments necessary to control and work with the problems we have created.

1. *Transportation.* More and more autos drive down our highways and city streets. In some cities, it takes longer to go by car from downtown to the airport than it does to take a 500-mile trip by air. Land

1

that could be used for housing or factories is being taken for freeways and parking lots. As suburbs move farther and farther from the center of the city, new ways have to be found to move people from home to work. Since more and more people are turning to air travel for longer journeys, air traffic has enormously increased. New terminals must be built and new methods devised to end the inconveniences and dangers of crowded skies.

2. *Air and water pollution.* Research has shown that the air we breathe is becoming increasingly contaminated with the waste matter from industry and motor vehicles. Similarly, many of our major streams and lakes have been polluted or are becoming dangerous to both man and animals.

3. *Housing.* The central sections of our cities are old and often dilapidated. Into these areas have flooded millions of recent migrants to the city. We are faced with the task of finding adequate, decent housing for these people. This job is made more difficult by the fact that a great many of the new migrants are Negro and Puerto Rican. Because of prejudice against them, language problems, and often a poor educational background, these people are unable to afford good housing outside the central city.

4. *Jobs.* In order to lead the good life, people need to work so that they can afford to buy what they want. Automation is eliminating many unskilled jobs, while new jobs are being created in skilled service industries. If our cities are to be healthy and prosperous, people must be able to obtain work.

5. *The quality of city life.* There is much talk about crime on the streets of our cities. Noise and dirt disturb the ears and the eyes. Historic old buildings are torn down and replaced by steel and glass. Educational excellence is merely a slogan in many big city schools. All of these things and many more cause concern about the general quality of life in our cities.

6. *Governmental institutions.* "Is it possible to really govern a big city?" The answer to this question seems to be yes, but more and more the big city's problems go beyond its borders. The need for rapid transit and for air pollution control are only examples of problems which affect the city and its surrounding area. Artificial political lines prevent a rational approach to many of the difficulties of urban life. New governmental arrangements are simply grafted onto those already in existence. The problems continue and grow worse.

7. *Urban area planning.* Many of America's cities have planning commissions whose job is to draw up a master plan for development of the city and to see that the plan is adhered to. We do not have metropolitan area planning commissions designed to plan for development of an entire area with common problems. The degree to which we are to rely on planning is a continuing issue in our nation. Some people claim

that planning lessens individual freedom of choice and is a threat to our free enterprise philosophy.

The listing of problems above does not exhaust the catalogue of woes faced by our cities. In a book of this size, it is impossible to cover adequately all of the dilemmas created by our increasing urbanization. The treatment here will deal primarily with the *ecology* of city life— the problems of our urban environment such as housing, pollution, and transportation—and with the creation of model cities which should allow all Americans to live the "good life."

It has been found in experiments conducted by psychologists that the amount of crowding and the general conditions of life have a profound impact on the functioning of animals. Emotional breakdowns become common when there is too much overcrowding; the ability to learn becomes stunted when animals live in isolation or deprivation. Man, too, needs a healthy environment if he is to be healthy. The remainder of this book will be a look in depth at some of the dilemmas mentioned above. The issues will be presented and then various opinions and facts will be given to provide you with some basis for discussion and for developing your own solutions.

2

The City: Past and Future

No one knows for certain when or how the first city developed. In all likelihood, it developed from an earlier, smaller settlement. But the city inevitably became something new and special in the human experience. A new dimension and scale was added to human life with the growth of cities.

The Greek philosopher Aristotle said of the city: "Men come together in the city to live; they remain there to live the good life." It is possible for men to live in cities when they are able to produce sufficient food so that some may specialize in other pursuits. A city arises when a group of nonagricultural specialists comes together and pools its various talents. One indispensable talent necessary for the growth and functioning of cities is writing. While a city may come into being without a writing system, it will not fully develop its administrative and legal system unless there is a system of writing.

The first cities probably developed about 5500 years ago in the Fertile Crescent, that area of present-day Iran which includes the valleys of the Tigris and Euphrates. Conditions in this area made city growth possible. There was a great deal of fertile land that could produce more than the farmers themselves could use. There was a natural transportation system, which meant that trade could take place and that people could get to the city. Because of the rivers the area had long been a meeting place for peoples of varying backgrounds, so there was an adequate store of ideas and skills to create a city.

The first cities, with names like Eridu, Erech, and Ur, were very much alike. Each of the cities was headed by a king, who was also the high priest. These high priest-kings had absolute power of life and death over their subjects.

At about this time, 3000 to 3500 B. C., man's technology (his means of production) underwent great changes, which lead to the growth of more and greater cities. The potter's wheel, the draw loom, the sailing vessel, copper metallurgy, the calendar, and writing all came into existence about this time. As the cities attracted more and more people, they became the scene of increased technological change. This led to greater division of labor among the residents. Cities began to expand and become empires.

The Greek city states are possibly the most famous of the old cities. Another famous city, Rome of the Roman Empire, at its height contained somewhere between 300,000 and 1,000,000 people. Rome was so crowded at one point that the officials had to issue special regulations concerning chariot traffic.

But the great explosion in the size of cities came with the industrial revolution. More specifically, it has come with the last 100 years of that revolution. All of the industrialized nations and many pre-industrial societies are experiencing or have experienced a tremendous growth in their cities. And the growth is continuing and increasing, along with a fantastic rise in the population of the world. This has created an urban problem of totally new proportions.

In the United States, the growth of cities was slow until the last half of the 19th Century. Then, fed by the increase in immigration from Europe and the movement of people from rural to urban areas, the cities began to grow rapidly.

Between 1840 and 1900, the population of New York City increased from 312,000 to 3,437,000. In the same time period, Chicago went from 4,000 people to 1,700,000. Boston, Philadelphia, and Pittsburgh had a similar growth. In the 85 years from 1880 to 1965, the population of Los Angeles soared from 10,000 to 2,276,-917.

It is not only the cities which have increased in size. The suburbs, particularly since World War II, have grown fantastically. Two examples will illustrate this trend:

· In 1947, the area which now houses Levittown, New York, had a single three-room schoolhouse with 37 pupils. By 1954, this six square miles housed 70,000 people, and the 37 pupils had increased by over 300 times, to 12,500.

· Daly City, California, which borders San Francisco on the south, had a population of about 10,000 people in 1940. By 1968, this had grown to over 67,000. San Mateo County, of which Daly City is a part, grew from 235,659 in 1950 to over 500,000 in 1968.

It is expected that by 1990 the population of this county will be over 900,000.

Suburbs are continuing to grow rapidly, but the growth of central cities has stopped and, in some cases (as shown by the chart below), they are losing citizens.

RANK 1965	CITY	POPULATION 1965	POPULATION 1940
1	New York, N. Y.	7,809,197	7,454,995
2	Chicago, Ill.	3,674,668	3,396,808
3	Los Angeles, Calif.	2,726,917	1,504,277
4	Philadelphia, Pa.	1,964,464	1,931,334
5	Detroit, Mich.	1,738,630	1,623,452
6	Houston, Texas	1,013,277	384,514
7	Baltimore, Md.	933,390	859,100
8	Cleveland, Ohio	924,233	878,336
9	Washington, D. C.	802,154	663,091
10	St. Louis, Missouri	768,777	816,048
11	Milwaukee, Wisc.	759,857	587,472
12	San Francisco, Calif.	755,122	634,536
13	Dallas, Texas	696,667	294,734
14	Boston, Mass.	683,253	770,816
15	New Orleans, La.	674,589	494,537
16	San Antonio, Texas	653,542	253,854
17	San Diego, Calif.	647,743	203,341
18	Phoenix, Ariz.	604,010	65,414
19	Pittsburgh, Pa.	570,489	671,659
20	Seattle, Wash.	563,215	368,302

It must be emphasized that urban growth is occurring around the world. Latin America and Africa, two continents which Americans usually think of as rural in their life style, are experiencing tremendous urban growth. This naturally causes great problems for the nations of these continents since many of them do not have the industrial capacity to supply jobs for all those who come to the city looking for work. On the outskirts of many Latin American cities there are huge shantytowns, where the newcomers try to survive.

The United States has always had mixed feelings about cities. On the one hand, some writers (such as Walt Whitman) have written of the virtues of the city; on the other, the vast majority of American writers and intellectuals has expressed a deep mistrust of the city. In general, this mistrust forms a theme in American life.

The poor girl goes to the city and is forced into a life of shame; the country hick goes to the city and is sold a bridge; or the honest young man from the country becomes an unhappy and destroyed city dweller.

These myths from the past are still important today. It is difficult for cities to get adequate legislation passed in state legislatures. The national Congress still overrepresents rural areas, so that city problems often go begging for solution. Recent events have brought some changes, but cities still find themselves at a disadvantage.

The following selections give some indication of the mixed feelings of Americans about the city.

1. THE VIEWS OF THOMAS JEFFERSON *

Jefferson saw the farmer—not the city worker—as the salvation of the nation. Would you agree with him?

Those who labor in the earth are the chosen people of God . . . Corruption of morals in the mass of cultivators is a phenomenon of which no age or nation has furnished an example . . . but, generally speaking, the proportion which the aggregate of the other classes of citizens bears in any state to that of its husbandmen, is the proportion of its unsound to its healthy parts, and is a good enough barometer whereby to measure its degree of corruption. . . . The mobs of great cities add just so much to the support of pure government, as sores do to the strength of the human body.

What Do You Think?

Fewer and fewer Americans live on farms (approximately eight per cent and declining). Does this mean that the nation's morality is being corrupted? Explain your answer.

---

* Excerpted from Dumas Malone, *Jefferson, the Virginian.* Boston, Mass.: Little, Brown & Co., 1948.

2. THE ROMANCE OF CITY LIFE *

The poet Walt Whitman looked at a city and saw something more than the mobs. His poem "Mannahatta" expresses this view.

I was asking for something specific and perfect for my city,
Whereupon lo! up sprang the aboriginal name.
Now I see what there is in a name, a word, liquid, sane, unruly, musical,
   self-sufficient,
I see that the word of my city is that word from of old,
Because I see that word nested in nests of water-bays superb,
Rich, hemm'd thick all around with sailships and steamships, an island
   sixteen miles long, solid-founded,
Numberless crowded streets, high growths of iron, slender, strong, light,
   splendidly uprising toward clear skies,
Tides swift and ample, well loved by me, toward sundown,
The flowing sea-currents, the little islands, larger adjoining islands, the
   heights, the villas,
The countless masts, the white shore-streamers, the lighters, the ferry-
   boats, the black sea-steamers well model'd,
The down-town streets, the jobbers' houses of business, the houses of
   business of the ship-merchants, and money-brokers, the river-streets,
Immigrants arriving, fifteen thousand in a week,
The carts hauling goods, the manly race of drivers of horses, the brown-
   faced sailors,
The summer air, the bright sun shining, and the sailing clouds aloft,
The winter snows, the sleigh-bells, the broken ice in the river, passing
   along up or down with the flood-tide or ebb-tide,
The mechanics of the city, the masters, well-form'd, beautiful-faced,
   looking you straight in the eyes,
Trottoirs throng'd, vehicles, Broadway, the women, the shops and shows,
A million people—manners free and superb—open voices—hospitality—
   the most courageous and friendly young men,
City of hurried and sparkling waters! City of spires and masts!
City nested in bays! My city!

---

* From Walt Whitman, "Mannahatta," in *Leaves of Green* (1855). New York,
N. Y.: New American Library, Mentor Edition.

1. Contrast Whitman's view with that of Jefferson. In what ways are they similar? Different? With whom would you agree? Explain.
2. Try to write a poem about your city or the city nearest you. If you can't write a poem, describe that city in several paragraphs.

3. PITY THE POOR COUNTRY GIRL *

Theodore Dreiser didn't trust the city any more than did Jefferson. Would a girl who moves to the city today face similar problems to those of Carrie?

When Caroline Meeber boarded the afternoon train for Chicago, her total outfit consisted of a small trunk, a cheap imitation alligator-skin satchel, a small lunch in a paper box, and a yellow leather snap purse, containing her ticket, a scrap of paper with her sister's address in VanBuren Street, and four dollars in money. It was August, 1889. She was eighteen years of age, bright, timid, and full of the illusions of ignorance and youth. Whatever touch of regret at parting characterized her thoughts, it was certainly not for advantages now being given up. A gush of tears at her mother's farewell kiss, a touch in her throat when the cars clacked by the flour mill where her father worked by the day, a pathetic sigh as the familiar green environs of the village passed in review, and the threads which bound her so lightly to girlhood and home were irretrievably broken.

To be sure there was always the next station, where one might descend and return. There was the great city, bound more closely by these very trains which came up daily. Columbia City was not so very far away, even once she was in Chicago. What, pray, is a few hours— a few hundred miles? She looked at the little slip bearing her sister's address and wondered. She gazed at the green landscape, now passing in swift review, until her swifter thoughts replaced its impression with vague conjectures of what Chicago might be.

When a girl leaves her home at eighteen, she does one of two things. Either she falls into saving hands and becomes better, or she

---

* Excerpted from Theodore Dreiser, *Sister Carrie* (1912). New York, N. Y.: Bantam Books.

rapidly assumes the cosmopolitan standard of virtue and becomes worse. Of an intermediate balance, under the circumstances, there is no possibility. The city has its cunning wiles, no less than the infinitely smaller and more human tempter.

There are large forces which allure with all the soulfulness of expression possible in the most cultured human. The gleam of a thousand lights is often as effective as the persuasive light in a wooing and fascinating eye. Half the undoing of the unsophisticated and natural mind is accomplished by forces wholly superhuman. A blare of sound, a roar of life, a vast array of human hives, appeal to the astonished senses in equivocal terms. Without a counsellor at hand to whisper cautious interpretations, what falsehoods may not these things breathe into the unguarded ear? Unrecognized for what they are, their beauty, like music, too often relaxes, then weakens, then perverts the simpler human perceptions.

What Do You Think?

From this short excerpt, what would you expect to be the future of Carrie Meeber in the big city? Explain.

4.   ARE WE OUR BROTHER'S KEEPER? *

Liverpool is not an American city, but the American writer Herman Melville felt moved to describe his experiences there. Similar conditions existed in some American cities in the mid-19th Century. Do conditions like these exist today anywhere? How could you find out?

In going to our boarding-house, the Sign of the Baltimore Clipper, I generally passed through a narrow street called "Launcelott's-Hey," lined with dingy, prison-like cotton warehouses. In this street, or rather alley, you seldom see any one but a truckman, or some solitary old warehouse-keeper, haunting his smoky den like a ghost.

Once, passing through this place, I heard a feeble wail, which seemed to come out of the earth. It was but a strip of crooked side-walk where I stood; the dingy wall was on every side, converting the mid-day into twilight; and not a soul was in sight. I started, and could almost have run, when I heard that dismal sound. At last I advanced to an opening which communicated downward with deep tiers of cellars

---

* Excerpted from Herman Melville, "The Shame of Liverpool," from *Redburn* (1859).

beneath a crumbling old warehouse; and there, some fifteen feet below the walk, crouching in the nameless squalor, with her head bowed over, the figure of what had been a woman. Her blue arms folded to her living bosom two shrunken things like children, that leaned toward her, one on each side. At first, I knew not whether they were alive or dead. They made no sign; they did not move or stir; but from the vault came the soul-sickening wail.

I made a noise with my foot, which, in the silence, echoed far and near; but there was no response. Louder still, when one of the children lifted its head, and cast upward a faint glance; then closed its eyes, and lay motionless. The woman also, now gazed up, and perceived me; but let fall her eye again. They were dumb and next to dead with want. How they had crawled into that den, I could not tell; but there they had crawled to die. At that moment I never thought of relieving them; for death was so stamped in their glazed and unimploring eyes, that I almost regarded them as already no more. I stood looking down on them, while my whole soul swelled within me; and I asked myself, What right had any body in the wide world to smile, and be glad, when sights like this were to be seen? . . .

At last, I walked on toward an open lot in the alley, hoping to meet there some ragged old women, whom I had daily noticed groping amid foul rubbish for little particles of dirty cotton, which they washed out and sold for a trifle.

I found them; and accosting one, I asked if she knew of the persons I had just left. She replied, that she did not; nor did she want to; I then asked another, a miserable, toothless old woman, with a tattered strip of coarse baling stuff round her body. Looking at me for an instant, she resumed her raking in the rubbish, and said that she knew who it was that I spoke of; but that she had no time to attend to beggars and their brats. Accosting still another, who seemed to know my errand, I asked if there was no place to which the woman could be taken. "Yes," she replied, "to the church-yard." I said she was alive, and not dead.

"Then she'll never die," was the rejoinder. "She's been down there these three days with nothing to eat; that I know myself." . . .

Leaving Launcelott's-Hey, I turned into a more frequented street; and soon meeting a policeman, told him of the condition of the woman and the girls.

"It's none of my business, Jack," said he. "I don't belong to that street."

Who does, then?"

"I don't know. But what business is it of yours? Are you not a Yankee?"

"Yes," said I, "but come, I will help you remove that woman, if you say so."

"There, now, Jack, go on board your ship and stick to it; leave these matters to the town."

I accosted two more policemen, but with no better success; they would not even go with me to the place. The truth was, it was out of the way, in a silent, secluded spot; and the misery of the three outcasts, hiding away in the ground, did not obtrude upon any one.

Returning to them, I again stamped to attract their attention; but this time none of the three looked up, or even stirred. While I yet stood irresolute, a voice called to me from a high, iron-shuttered window in a loft over the way; and asked what I was about. I beckoned to the man, a sort of porter, to come down, which he did; when I pointed down into the vault.

"Well," said he, "what of it?"

"Can't we get them out?" said I, "haven't you some place in your warehouse where you can put them? Have you nothing for them to eat?"

"You're crazy, boy," said he; "do you suppose that Parkins and Wood want their warehouse turned into a hospital?"

I then went to my boarding-house, and told Handsome Mary of what I had seen; asking her if she could not do something to get the woman and girls removed; or if she could not do that, let me have some food for them. But though a kind person in the main, Mary replied that she gave away enough to beggars in her own street (which was true enough) without looking after the whole neighborhood.

Going into the kitchen, I accosted the cook, a little shriveled-up old Welshwoman with a saucy tongue, whom the sailors called Brandy-Nan; and begged her to give me some cold victuals, if she had nothing better, to take to the vault. But she broke out in a storm of swearing at the miserable occupants of the vault, and refused. I then stepped into the room where our dinner was being spread; and waiting till the girl had gone out, I snatched some bread and cheese from a stand, and thrusting it into the bosom of my frock, left the house. Hurrying to the lane, I dropped the food down into the vault. One of the girls caught at it convulsively, but fell back, apparently fainting; the sister pushed the other's arm aside, and took the bread in her hand; but with a weak uncertain grasp like an infant's. She placed it to her mouth; but letting it fall again, murmuring faintly something like "water." The woman did not stir; her head was bowed over, just as I had first seen her.

Seeing how it was, I ran down toward the docks to a mean little sailor tavern, and begged for a pitcher; but the cross old man who kept it refused, unless I would pay for it. But I had no money. So as my boarding-house was some way off, and it would be lost time to run to the ship for my big iron pot; under the impulse of the moment, I hurried to one of the Boodle Hydrants, which I remembered having seen running near the scene of a still smoldering fire in an old rag house; and taking off a new tarpaulin hat, which had been loaned me that day, filled it with water.

With this, I returned to Launcelott's-Hey; and with considerable difficulty, like getting down into a well, I contrived to descend with it into the vault; where there was hardly enough space left to let me stand. The two girls drank out of the hat together; looking up at me with an unalterable, idiotic expression, that almost made me faint. The woman spoke not a word, and did not stir. . . .

I crawled up into the street, and looking down on them again, almost repented that I had brought them any food; for it would only tend to prolong their misery, without hope of any permanent relief, for die they must very soon; they were too far gone for any medicine to help them. I hardly know whether I ought to confess another thing that occurred to me as I stood there; but it was this—I felt an almost terrible impulse to do them the last mercy, of in some way putting an end to their horrible lives; and I should almost have done so, I think, had I not been deterred by thoughts of the law. For I well knew that the law, which would let them perish of themselves without giving them one cup of water, would spend a thousand pounds, if necessary, in convicting him who should do so much as offer to relieve them from their miserable existence. . . .

I could do no more . . . being obliged to repair to the ship; but at twelve o'clock, when I went to dinner, I hurried into Launcelott's-Hey, when I found that the vault was empty. In place of the woman and children, a heap of quick-lime was glistening. I could not learn who had taken them away, or whither they had gone; but my prayer was answered —they were dead, departed, and at peace.

But again I looked down into the vault, and in fancy beheld the pale, shrunken forms still crouching there. Ah! what are our creeds, and how do we hope to be saved? Tell me, oh Bible, that story of Lazarus again that I may find comfort in my heart for the poor and forlorn. Surrounded as we are by the wants and woes of our fellow-men, and yet given to follow our own pleasures, regardless of their pains, are we not like people sitting up with a corpse, and making merry in the house of the dead?

What Do You Think?

Reread the final paragraph. What is your reaction to that paragraph? Does it hold true for us today? Explain.

5. IS MAN THE KEY TO THE PROBLEM? *

Former head of the United States Department of Housing and Urban Development Robert Weaver suggests that the crucial element in the problems of the city is human behavior. Would you agree?

Cities have always been threatened. A few, like Pompeii, have been wiped out by natural forces. Others have suffered from destruction by man. Human enemies from without and dissension and revolution from within have frequently destroyed or captured and transformed them. They have always been harassed by social problems. For centuries some men have considered cities as centers of evil and sought to destroy this symbol. More recently, we have been told that many urban residents develop guilt feelings about their association with cities. Thus, the recent escape to suburbia may have deep historical and psychological roots. Be that as it may, when technology perfected means of mass transportation, man was able to participate in the city's economic activities at the same time that he centered his family life beyond its borders. Once this occurred, a new concept of urban life, a central city with suburban satellites, developed. The metropolitan area became a reality, and with its rise there appeared a new cluster of urban problems.

In all of the city's problems, the key element has been human beings. People conceived and developed cities. People have constantly threatened them. People, congregating into urban centers, made them the complex social organism we contemplate when the word city is used. It is human beings who, today, are shaping the vast metropolitan areas which house some two-thirds of the population in this Nation. Consequently, it is in terms of people that urban problems must be conceived and their solutions developed.

What Do You Think?

1. Weaver states that "it is in terms of people that urban problems must be conceived and their solutions developed." Would you agree or disagree? Give your reasons.
2. What reasons for the growth of suburban living does Weaver give? Do you agree or disagree with him? Why?

---

* Abridged from *The Urban Complex* by Robert C. Weaver. Copyright 1955, 1959 by Atlanta University; Copyright 1960 by the Academy of Political Science; Copyright 1964 by Wayne State University; Copyright 1960, 1961, 1963, 1964 by Robert C. Weaver. Used by permission of Doubleday & Co., Inc.

6.   AN OVERVIEW OF THE PROBLEM *

*Our metropolitan areas are growing, and their problems are growing
faster than they are. The selection which follows points out some
reasons for the problems and gives an overview of the current situation. Given the problems set forth, can our cities survive?*

"The approved way to talk about cities these days," says Paul
Ylisaker of the Ford Foundation, "is to speak solemnly, sadly, and
fearfully about their problems. You don't rate as an expert on the city
unless you foresee its doom . . . As a matter of fact, it probably died
yesterday."

There is ample cause for the doomsaying that washes over our cities
today. Every metropolitan center has its own catalogue of crises—but
the list reads much the same whether the city be Chicago or Atlanta,
New York or Los Angeles. The list: spreading slums, declining downtown,
polluted air and water, car-clogged streets, inadequate parks, high crime
rates, bulging welfare rolls, crowded and underfinanced schools, racial
problems, incessant demands for more services, and soaring costs for
everything. Compounding the difficulties which local officials face in
trying to cope with these problems is the fact that most cities are
desperately short of money.

The title of one of this year's crop of books on the urban dilemma
echoes the prevailing attitude: *Sick Cities.* The author, Gordon Mitchell,
contends that the nation's major metropolises may be turning into urban
dinosaurs—the implication, of course, is that cities might be heading
for extinction, too.

So complex do the problems of the older central cities seem that
some observers go so far as to suggest that they be abandoned, and
in their place new, carefully planned small towns (interspersed with
parkland) be built. . . .

Yet somewhere in the preface to the catalogue of urban ills, perhaps
here, should be a footnote to the effect that cities do have their good
points. After all, they spill across more land, and embrace a greater
percentage of the American population every year. This fact, sometimes
mislaid amid the prophesies of doom and gloom, has prompted Ylisaker,
for one, to wonder whether it wasn't about time we began to view the
city less as a set of problems than as a very substantial human success.

---

* Abridged and reprinted by permission of Scholastic Magazine, Inc., from
Senior Scholastic, "The City in the '60's—Doomed by Some, Defended by
Others," October 11, 1963. Copyright 1965 by Scholastic Magazines, Inc.

Despite high rents and traffic jams, cities have long beckoned to the adventurous and the ambitious. They have always been the centers of business and learning, government and the arts. Such centers are natural magnets. This has been true since urban civilization began, and it remains true in . . . America [today]. For every expert who cries "doom!" there is a confirmed city dweller who wouldn't dream of living anywhere else and who pities those who do. As a German observer of the urban scene, Wolf Schneider, puts it: "Wherever many people are, the great events take place."

The U. S. becomes more urbanized every year, even as the old distinctions between "city" and "country" blur. The 1960 census indicates that seven of every 10 persons live in an "urban household," a complete reversal of the findings of the first U. S. census in 1790 —when only one in 20 Americans lived in an "urban place." In the decade from 1951 to 1960, 84 per cent of the nation's total population growth occurred in "standard metropolitan areas." (A standard metropolitan area is defined as a county or group of contiguous counties containing at least one city of 50,000 or more plus an outlying area that is somewhat urban in character.) Between 1951 and 1960 the population of the nation's 212 metropolitan areas rose from 87,597,000 to 108,- 873,000, and is still soaring.

While the metropolitan areas as a whole have been expanding— both in size and in population—the population within the areas has been shifting. Collectively, the suburbs grew six times faster than their parent cities in the 10 years before the 1960 census. The two largest cities, New York and Chicago, actually lost population within their legal city limits. Their suburbs grew, and with them the core cities' problems. "The city today, for many, spells crime, dirt, and race tensions more than it does culture and opportunity. While some people still escape from the small town to the city, still more are escaping from the city to the suburbs." Thus David Riesman, writing in the *Annals of the American Political Science Association,* sums up the situation.

From every large American city the more prosperous citizens have surged outward, seeking open space and suburban amenities. Oversimplified, the "flight to the suburbs" follows this pattern: the young middle-class family decides to move to the suburbs "for the children," but the father still commutes back to the core city for work. While in the city, he requires such municipal services as police and fire protection, and street maintenance. Such services he has always required, but now there is a key difference—he is no longer paying his share toward providing them, since his property tax (the biggest source of local revenue) now goes to the suburb where he lives. Exit one more source of revenue for the core city, and one more socially responsible, law-abiding family.

Meanwhile, back in the old neighborhood, there arrives a newcomer

—often from a rural area of another city, generally poor, generally unskilled. He comes seeking work, but it is scarce. To meet the rent, two or more families crowd into the space formerly occupied by a single family. Plaster starts to crumble. It is not fixed. Paint peels. It is not renewed. As more and more unskilled, unemployed people jam into the neighborhood, whole blocks turn dingy and overcrowded. Garbage accumulates, luring rats and bugs.

In place of a tax-producing, socially responsible neighborhood, there is now a crowded slum—filled with children who must be provided with schools, unskilled individuals and broken families who swell the welfare rolls, unlawful elements who require more police, and decrepit buildings that are fire hazards. The section has become a liability to the city, both in terms of cost and in terms of human waste it represents.

Yet this isn't a problem of the 1960's alone. Back in 1870, New York City residents were already fretting because men of "moderate income" were hieing themselves to the "suburban towns." A writer of the time said that with its "middle class in large part self-exiled, its laboring population being brutalized in the tenements, and its citizens of the highest class indifferent to the common weal, New York has drifted from bad to worse and become the prey of professional thieves, ruffians, and political jugglers." That was 93 years ago. It sounds very much like a commentary on contemporary big city life.

A recent study of who is leaving the cities and who is arriving described the migrants from the older core cities today as predominantly "urban, middle- and upper-income whites," while the incoming group was "largely rural, low-income blacks."

Writing in *Fortune,* Charles Silberman argues that the city is in trouble because it is no longer dealing successfully with its newcomers. "They are still pouring in—not from County Cork, or Bavaria, or Sicily, or Galacia, *but* from Jackson, Mississippi, and Memphis, Tennessee, and a host of towns and hamlets . . . The new immigrants (to the North) are distinguished from the older residents not by religion or national origin, but by color."

Between 1950 and 1960, the 12 largest U. S. cities lost over 2,000,000 white residents. They gained nearly 2,000,000 Negro residents. Any shift of this magnitude would strain the social fabric of the cities affected, but with the additional complications caused by racial attitudes, the problems quadruple.

Since 1949, when the Federal Housing Act was passed, federal funds have been available to cities trying to "renew" their blighted areas. The cities had their own projects going before that, but the availability of federal funds has spurred the process.

In most urban renewal projects, the city condemns and buys the blighted area. The land is then cleared and made available at reduced prices to developers who rebuild it. It is not always put back into housing—sometimes the cleared area becomes a civic center, or a commercial area.

While some strikingly successful public projects have been built, the process is extremely costly, and often involves dislocating large numbers of people who must be rehoused while the slum they occupied is razed or rehabilitated. Often the displaced slumites spill into nearby areas, creating a new slum just as the old one disappears. In recent years, in fact, the spread of new slums has galloped ahead of attempts to erase the old ones.

Some public housing units built in urban renewal efforts have been widely and bitterly criticized for their barracks-like appearance, and for the dullness of their architecture. They lack all the variety that makes city life interesting, critics say.

Nevertheless, there are increasing calls for massive government support for slum clearance. One long-time supporter of slum clearance, Charles F. Palmer of Atlanta, Georgia, noted that in 1962 more Americans lived in slums than on farms. "The slum problem has taken a back seat too long," Palmer says. "With a couple of million fewer farmers than slumites, our federal expenditure per farm family is $3,000 per year against $84 per slum family." Palmer estimates that 22,000,000 people live in slums, requiring construction of 5,000,000 new public housing units.

Most authorities today argue that a high degree of large-scale planning is the only way to stop the spread of urban blight, and to rejuvenate the central core of cities. "It is obvious that unplanned, uncoordinated, unguided, and uncontrolled urban growth has not solved any of the problems occasioned by explosive urbanization," says a Florida urban planner.

The German writer Schneider agrees that some master plan is essential if cities are not to suffocate and be over-run with cars and trucks. Residents will have to invest billions in well-considered rehabilitation programs, he says. And, while he does caution every city planner to be aware that many of the things people like in cities can develop far better without planning, he nevertheless argues that urban planners should be given vast sums of money, and the freedom to implement their designs.

There are others, however, who object vigorously to large-scale efforts to remodel their cities according to some expert's plan. Sometimes the attack centers in a suggestion to "renew" a favorite neighborhood.

"A metropolis is a million odds and ends, mainly odds, that can never be filtered through a concrete box and come out all pink and white and smelling of Arpège," writes San Francisco *Chronicle* columnist Herb Caen. "Let the city stay free and wild. Let there be funny old houses for funny young people, and ugly old buildings bursting with life.

When every building on the hill looks like the one next to it, it will not be San Francisco."

Sometimes the critics of planning attack the whole notion that experts with trucks full of money can map out an ideal city. "There is a wistful myth," writes Jane Jacobs, a New York author and architectural critic, "if we only had enough money to spend—the figure is usually put at a hundred billion dollars—we could wipe out all slums in 10 years, reverse decay . . . anchor the wandering middle class . . . and perhaps even solve the traffic problem. But look what we have built with the first several billions: low-income projects that become worse centers of delinquency, vandalism, and general social helplessness than the slums they were supposed to replace. Middle-income projects which are truly marvels of dullness and regimentation . . . This is not the rebuilding of cities. This is the *sacking* of cities!"

What Do You Think?

1.   If our population continues to expand, what would you expect to be the future of essential services in metropolitan areas? How would you solve the problem of costs for these services?

2.   "Yes," say some, "cities are a problem but name a better way for people to live." Go ahead, name *your* better way.

7.   IS IT POSSIBLE TO GOVERN NEW YORK? *

Some people maintain that the big city has outgrown its usefulness and that the solution lies in smaller units. In the biggest of the big cities, New York, the problems facing the mayor have prompted the question of whether it is possible to govern a city of this size. Here are some of Mayor John Lindsay's views:

Our cities exact too much from those who live in them. They are not only increasingly expensive places in which to live or work; more and more, the price of city living is being paid by a sacrifice of fundamental personal freedoms.

Freedom to use the sidewalks and parks at night without fear.

Freedom to rent an apartment or buy a house at a reasonable cost.

Freedom to send children to school with the knowledge the class-

---

* Excerpted from John V. Lindsay, "The Future of the American City," *Saturday Review*, January, 1966. Copyright 1966 Saturday Review, Inc.

rooms will be bright and clean, the teachers skilled, and the instruction challenging.

Freedom to find a job or join a union without being frustrated by racial or religious discrimination.

Freedom to move about the city with reasonable speed and convenience on a public transportation system.

Freedom to breathe the air and use the waterways with equanimity.

City residents must, of course, adjust to some impositions to gain the varied advantages of urban living. Crowds, noise and rush, for example, are natural components of the city's pervasive excitement. But most of our major cities offer more liabilities than attractions. They have not succeeded in providing environments that meet ordinary standards of pleasure and comfort because they have not learned how to cope with the basic urban problems that vitiate our amenities and our liberties. The failure, however, is not uniform; every American city can learn from the individual successes of others.

Chicago, for example, reduced its crime rate for two consecutive years by tripling the number of patrol cars, speeding up communications, and eliminating redundant paperwork.

Pittsburgh marshaled its business community to overcome its once legendary air pollution problem. Los Angeles took extraordinary but practical steps to ensure its water supply. Philadelphia has led in rehabilitation slum housing, St. Louis in waterfront development, and San Francisco in the planning of a unified, area transportation system.

The specific routes to these accomplishments cannot always be followed by other cities. But they deserve rigorous inspection and evaluation. . . .

The real barriers to the workable, enjoyable city, however, are frustration, despair and cynicism. I believe they can be surmounted by creating a city government created by staffing City Hall with the finest talent, the most dedicated professionals, and the keenest minds, without obeisance to party affiliations. Cities should abandon the petty self-defeating practice of trying to operate with an officialdom expediently drawn from relatives, precinct captains, special interest groups, campaign contributors and party hacks. The invariably tragic result is to render it impossible to attract into city government the men and women of excellence the city vitally needs; they may sacrifice top salaries and normal hours to serve their city, but they will not relinquish their pride to an administration with a vision curtailed by the next election date.

It is not enough, however, to rest on the basically inner-directed concept of attracting the best administrators. City Hall must extend itself to the residents of the city whose only personal contact with their government often takes the form of a policeman, a housing inspector, or an ambulance driver. The widespread estrangement—often a pronounced alienation—that characterizes the relationship between a city government and its citizens can be bridged by granting people a strong, direct voice in the affairs of their city. Mayors might explore the establishment of neighborhood offices throughout their cities to give residents a line into City Hall when they want answers or action on such perennial problems as better street lights, smoke abatement, vandalism, landlord-tenant disputes, and enforcement of dog leash laws. The immediate objective would be to obtain results on sensible requests and justifiable complaints. . . .

These will be adventurous years in American cities, for in their span we shall do much to decide whether major cities will rise proudly at the center or disintegrate at the core of our intensely populated and still expanding urban complexes. The outcome will be crucially important, for the issue in the struggle to achieve livable cities is not only the nature of our increasingly urban society, but the nature of our future civilization.

What Do You Think?

1. Some people would say that Lindsay is optimistic. Do you think he is or not? Give some evidence which substantiates your belief.
2. Mayor Lindsay mentions several cities which have solved very difficult problems. Investigate these cities and see if they have actually done all that Lindsay indicates they have done.

ACTIVITIES FOR INVOLVEMENT

1. As the chapter points out, there are many different ways of looking at the city. Historically we have viewed it as both a "slough of despond" and a great center of opportunity. Arrange a debate among members of the class on the question, Resolved: That the American city is the hope of our future.

2. Form a small committee to arrange a visit to City Hall. It would be wise to arrange in advance for interviews with those people you wish to see. Attempt to find out the answer to the question: Is it possible to govern this city? If you find that the answer you are given, or the answer that you personally arrive at, is "no," attempt to create a new plan for government or a new form of living arrangement other than the city. Present your paper to the class for discussion.

3. Man and his habits are a large part of the city's problem. Make a list of man's habits that make the city a good place to live, and a contrasting list of his habits that make it an unpleasant place. How could you change some of the harmful habits?

4. Write your own view of your city. Let your imagination go and

attempt to capture whatever it is that makes your city an exciting and dynamic place. If you find it otherwise, try to capture this also.

5.   Listed below are a number of words that writers have used to describe the city. Which do you think are most appropriate? Least? Why?

exciting	dying	dirty
ugly	moving	golden
sick	warm	turbulent
electric	alive	hard
vibrant	cold	frightening

What words would you add to the list? How would you describe the city in a few sentences?

3

Slums and Suburbs: Two Nations— Divisible

Every large city in the United States has its slums—sections of older, deteriorating housing. And there are rural slums, too. These are the shantytowns, often populated by migrant farm workers or others who have been cut off from the affluence that characterizes middle-class life in America.

In the cities, slums are caused by many factors. Increasing age of buildings, failure on the part of landowners to keep up their property, the desire for maximum profit which impels landlords to subdivide homes into apartments, the processes of racial discrimination which force black people to live in ghettos owned by whites who care little for the nature of the community they are helping to create—all help to cause our slums.

Providing adequate housing for the nation has been an issue in this country for a long time. In 1939, Congress passed the Federal Housing Authority Act, which provided a federal guarantee for mortgages. The G. I. Bill of Rights in World War II provided for low-interest loans to veterans of the war. Korean and Vietnam veterans also earned such rights. Immense amounts of housing have been built since the war to accommodate the increased population. But most of this housing has been built in suburban areas, and little of it has gone to the poor. Only 650,000 units of federally sponsored public housing have been built in the nation. Urban renewal programs aimed at destroying the slums have earned the nickname "Negro removal," for often low-priced housing has been replaced with middle- and upper-priced housing which the people who lived in the area before the renewal cannot afford.

In 1968 Congress passed a new housing bill aimed at remedying some of these ills. It remains to be seen whether or not the appropriation will be sufficient to deal with the problem. In the meantime, people will continue to live under conditions such as those described in the readings that follow.

1. SLUMS ARE NOT NEW TO OUR NATION *

The fight against our slums has been a long one and, as the following reading shows, people in the past have thought the battle was won. How would you respond to this author?

The slum complaint had been chronic in all ages, but the great changes which the nineteenth century saw, the new industry, political freedom, brought on an acute attack which threatened to become fatal. Too many of us had supposed that, built as our commonwealth was on universal suffrage, it would be proof against the complaints that harassed older states; but in fact it turned out that there was extra hazard in that. Having solemnly resolved that all men are created equal and have certain inalienable rights, among them life, liberty, and the pursuit of happiness, we shut our eyes and waited for the formula to work. . . .

So the battle began. . . . [T]he civic conscience awoke in 1879.

In that year the slum was arraigned in the churches. The sad and shameful story was told of how it grew and was fostered by avarice that saw in the homeless crowds from over the sea only a chance for business and exploited them to the uttermost, making sometimes a hundred per cent on the capital invested—always most out of the worst houses, from the tenants of which "nothing was expected" save that they pay the usurious rents—how Christianity, citizenship, human fellowship, shook their skirts clear of the rabble that was only good enough to fill the greedy purse, and how the rabble, left to itself, improved such opportunities as it found after such fashion as it knew; how it ran elections merely to count its thugs in, and fattened at the public crib; and how the whole evil thing had its root in the tenements, where the home had ceased to be sacred—those dark and deadly dens in which the family ideal was tortured to death and character was smothered, in which children were "damned rather than born" into the world, thus realizing a slum kind of foreordination to torment, happily brief in many cases. The Tenement House Committee long afterward called the worst of

---

* Excerpted from Jacob A. Riis, "The Battle with the Slum," *Jubilee—One Hundred Years of the Atlantic*. Boston, Mass.: Little, Brown & Co., 1957.

the barracks "infant slaughterhouses," and showed, by reference to the mortality lists, that they killed one in every five babies born in them.

The story shocked the town into action. Plans for a better kind of tenement were called for, and a premium was put on every ray of light and breath of air that could be let into it. Money was raised to build model houses, and a bill to give the health authorities summary powers in dealing with tenements was sent to the legislature. The landlords held it up until the last day of the session, when it was forced through by an angered public opinion. The power of the cabal was broken. The landlords had found their Waterloo. Many of them got rid of their property, which in a large number of cases they had never seen, and tried to forget the source of their ill-gotten wealth. Light and air did find their way into the tenements in a halfhearted fashion, and we began to count the tenants as "souls." That is one of our milestones in the history of New York. They were never reckoned so before; no one ever thought of them as "souls." So, restored to human fellowship, in the twilight of the air shaft that had penetrated to their dens, the first Tenement House Committee was able to make them out "better than the houses" they lived in, and a long step forward was taken. The Mulberry Bend, the wicked core of the "bloody Sixth Ward," was marked for destruction, and all slumdom held its breath to see it go. With that gone, it seemed as if the old days must be gone too, never to return. . . .

The streets are cleaned; the slum has been washed. Even while I am writing, a bill is urged in the legislature to build in every senatorial district in the city a gymnasium and a public bath. It matters little whether it passes at this session or not. The important thing is that it is there. The rest will follow. A people's club is being organized to crowd out the saloon that has had a monopoly of the brightness and the cheer in the tenement streets too long. The labor unions are bestirring themselves to deal with the sweating curse, and the gospel of less law and more enforcement sits enthroned at Albany. Theodore Roosevelt will teach us again Jefferson's forgotten lesson, that "the whole art of government consists in being honest."

One after another, the outworks of the slum have been taken. The higher standards now set up on every hand, in the cleaner streets, in the better schools, in the parks and the clubs, in the settlements, and in the thousand and one agencies for good that touch and help the lives of the poor at as many points, will tell at no distant day and react upon the homes and upon their builders. Philanthropy is not sitting idle and waiting. It is building tenements on the human plan that lets in sunshine and air and hope. It is putting up hotels deserving of the name for the army that just now had no other home than the cheap lodging houses which Inspector Byrnes firmly called "nurseries of crime." These are standards from which there is no backing down, and they are here to stay, for they pay. That is the test. Not charity, but justice—that is the gospel which they preach.

What Do You Think?

1. Mr. Riis is very optimistic in his conclusion, written before the 20th Century had begun. Write a letter to Mr. Riis in which you point out to him how his dreams have been realized or how the city has failed to live up to his expectations.

2. The author thinks that dealing with the slum is a matter of justice. What does he mean by this? What type of justice is he talking about?

3. Do you think there would be the same kind of opposition today to clearing up the slums that there was in the late 19th Century? Defend your position on this question.

2. A COMMUNITY IS MORE THAN BUILDINGS *

Harrison Salisbury of The New York Times *has spent years in the Soviet Union. Here are some of his comments on public housing there and in America. Are these judgments valid?*

New brick towers rise along the right-of-way of the New York Central and the New Haven as the commuting trains sweep down from Connecticut and Westchester. The men from Wall Street sometimes talk about it as they fold away the *Times* and the *Tribune* and prepare to get off at Grand Central. It is remarkable, they say, the progress which is being made in the city. You can hardly recognize Harlem. The East Side has been transformed.

Driving out the Gowanus Super-Highway they admire the rectangular patterns of Fort Greene Houses, Gowanus Houses, Red Hook Houses, Queensbridge Houses. It makes you feel good, they say, to live in a country where progress happens almost overnight. Of course, they do not agree with some of the things that are being done in Washington but you have to admit that people are better taken care of than in the

---

* Excerpted from *The Shook-up Generation,* by Harrison Salisbury. New York, N. Y.: Harper & Row, 1958. Copyright 1958 by Harrison Salisbury. Pp 73–79. Reprinted by permission of Harper & Row, Publishers.

old days. Maybe they are treated too well. It just encourages more of them to come up from Puerto Rico and the Deep South.

This is how people talk. I know because this is the way I talked until recently. I have been away from the United States a good deal since the war. When I came back to New York and drove the expressway around the island I hardly recognized parts of the city. The great experiment in public housing launched during the Roosevelt administration seemed to have paid off. I was amazed at the changes. Whole areas of the city had given way to fine new construction. I wished that I could take a delegation of Russians around and show them what a magnificent job we were doing in the field of public housing.

Then, last winter I visited Fort Greene Houses, Brooklyn. I was warned that most visitors preferred to walk up three or four flights instead of taking the elevator. I quickly understood why they chose the steep, cold staircases rather than face the stench of stale urine that pervades the elevators.

Until my nostrils ferreted out the fetid story of Fort Greene and until I had seen the inside of Marcy Houses and St. Nicholas Houses, I was not aware that in too many instances we have merely institutionalized our slums. We have immured old horror and new deprivation behind these cold walls.

I saw shoddy housing in Moscow. Many Soviet apartment houses are built so cheaply and maintained so badly that you cannot guess from looking whether they are two years old or twenty. I have seen Moscow elevators that don't work and Moscow plumbing that stinks. But until I visited Greene I had never seen elevators used by children as public toilets. I never imagined that I could find the equivalent of Moscow's newly built slums in the United States. But I have made the unfortunate discovery at Fort Greene and other places. The same shoddy shiftlessness, the broken windows, the missing light bulbs, the plaster cracking from the walls, the pilfered hardware, the cold, drafty corridors, the doors on sagging hinges, the acid smell of sweat and cabbage, the ragged children, the plaintive women, the playgrounds that are seas of muddy clay, the bruised and battered trees, the ragged clumps of grass, the planned absence of art, beauty or taste, the gigantic masses of brick, of concrete, of asphalt, the inhuman genius with which our know-how has been perverted to create human cesspools worse than those of yesterday.

If these words seem strong, visit these massive barracks for the destitute yourself. Visit Fort Greene with its thirty-four hundred families —possibly seventeen thousand people. It is described as the world's largest housing project. It is better described as a $20,000,000 slum.

This situation would be bad if it were unavoidable and irremediable. It is neither. It was created by the perversion, part accidental, part deliberate, of a well-intended effort to eliminate a sordid, social evil, the old slum. Many of these conditions are caused by blind enforcement of bureaucratic rules. Others stem from inadequate concepts, bad administration and, often, deliberate sabotage by cruel, stupid and heartless men. Some projects seem more like Golgothas designed to twist, torture and destroy the hapless people condemned to their dismal precincts than new homes for misfortunates. None of this is necessary. All of it could have been avoided.

Not all low-cost housing projects are like Fort Greene. Some are as good as you could wish. All have been founded in noble and high intent. But in practice Fort Greene and some others have been turned into monsters, devouring their residents, polluting the areas around them, spewing out a social excrescence which infects the whole of our society. The damage is not confined to New York. The violence loosed by Fort Greene sets in motion a wave of adolescent conflict which is borne from one end of the nation to the other.

Admission to low-rent projects, in New York City, basically is determined by income levels. The lower the income the higher the priority. Charity, welfare and relief cases get first choice. No discrimination for color, creed, or race is permitted. Or such is the pleasant theory. Actually, the sharp knife of poverty discriminates far more effectively than a *numerus clausus*. The rules tend to make ghettos of color and race out of the huge aggregates in which one family out of twenty in New York City now lives.

In the last seven years 300,000 Puerto Ricans have migrated to New York. In the same period perhaps 300,000 Negroes have come in. A high percentage of these people are in the bottom income category. Many are jobless. They go on welfare. The transition from the barrios of Puerto Rico to the factories of New York is not always so easy.

Because of their social and economic need, these people receive preference in public housing. There is nothing wrong about this. Public housing is subsidized by the state for the specific purpose of helping low-income groups. But indiscriminate application of this means test populates Fort Greene or Red Hook almost exclusively with that segment of the population which is least capable of caring for itself—economically, socially, culturally.

The concentration of the ill, the halt and the crippled (socially or physically) increase constantly because when a family's income rises to a minimum figure it must leave the project. The able, rising families are driven out month after month as their wages cross the ceiling mark. At the intake the economic and social levels drop lower and lower as inflation waters down the fixed-income limit and depression bites away at employment. It is the new unskilled immigrant from Mississippi or San Juan who first loses his job, goes on relief, and is put at the top of the waiting list for low-cost housing.

In some New York housing projects the majority of the families are welfare cases. At Red Hook Houses, relief cases constitute 25 per cent of the twenty-nine hundred families in the project. By screening the applicants to eliminate those with even modest wages the project community is systematically deprived of the normal quota of human talents needed for self-organization, self-discipline and self-improvement. It becomes a catch basin for the dregs of society. It lacks capability to help itself. It breeds endless social ills. It constitutes an ever-replenishing vessel for trouble. It is a built-in consumer of limitless social assistance.

The trouble starts long before the prisonlike towers and blocks of Fort Greene or Marcy Houses begin to fill up with socially deprived people. It starts when slum clearance begins.

The stated objective of slum clearance is to clean out a section of the city which has decayed, to tear down dilapidated, rat-infested tenements, to wipe out the debris-filled "home" workshops, obliterate the dives, the dens, the cribs and the blind pigs.

The concept is a little like that of a dentist. Drill out the infected cavity and fill it with nice new wholesome cement. It may hurt a little at first but the end justifies the pain. However, the slum clearer is not a dentist. His drill uproots all the people in the neighborhood, good as well as bad. He tears down the churches. He destroys local business. He sends the neighborhood lawyer to new offices downtown. The clinic and the synagogue move to the Bronx.

Bulldozers do not understand that a community is more than broken-down buildings and dirty storefronts. It is a tight skein of human relations. It has a life all its own. The wreckers tear this human fabric to ribbons. The old-timers are driven from their run-down flats and their ancient brick houses. They cannot wait three years for the new houses to open. Nothing more than a passing effort is made to give them a place in the new building anyway. They need a place to live here and now. So they drift away. They find a worse flat in a tumble-down on the edge of the new ghetto-to-be. They go their way, resentful, bitter, lives twisted out of joint. The new neighborhood can never be as good as the old, or so they think.

What Do You Think?

1. Salisbury describes conditions which exist. Yet, he says, they need not exist. If you had had the power, what would you have done to prevent these conditions from arising?

2. The author says there is something wrong with having the poor unfortunate live in a single area. What do you feel about this? Why?

3.   SLUM RESIDENTS SPEAK OUT *

The following represents testimony before the United States Commission on Civil Rights in 1967. All of the speakers in the first section are describing life as they know it—in Cleveland, Ohio; Gary, Indiana; or Boston, Massachusetts.

"The apartment was very dirty, an undecorated apartment. The plaster in the bathroom was all cracked up . . . and the bathtub, the water dropped by drops, just a drop at a time."

"They move to a building that is a little bit bettter, a building in which the plumbing is a little less bad, a building in which maybe the roof doesn't leak or a building where you do have some type of toilet facilities. So nobody wants this [deteriorated] building and they left because it is even worse than the one to which they moved. God knows that is bad enough, so it stands there. The landlord won't do anything with it and the city won't do anything with it. It just stands there . . ."

(Q) "Are rats a problem in your neighborhood?"

(A) "Yes, they are. I was living in one apartment, the rats got in bed with me, and my sister is still living in the same building and the rats are jumping up and down. The kids they play with rats like a child would play with a dog or something. They chase them around the house and things like this."

"I'll tell you when you start complaining about that particular building, no one seems to want to own the building. When I first started to complain. I started with one realty company and I complained so long and loud they sent someone else out and when I complained to him and they sent someone else out . . . Now we complain—it's five of us are complaining now . . . The only time anybody really wants the building is when it is time to pay the rent and after that nobody wants the building."

[The story is little different in Gary, Indiana.]

"Most of the apartments are just rooms. Very few of them have complete baths and hot and cold water, the necessary things, the things that are required healthwise they don't have, very few of them, hot and cold water, heat and this type of thing. You just don't find too many apartments in this area that have this type of thing."

---

* Excerpted from *A Time to Listen . . . A Time to Act. A Report of the National Advisory Commission on Civil Rights, 1967.*

"I mean outside of this district time marches on . . . They build better and they have better but you come down here and you see the same thing year after year after year. People struggling, people wanting, people needing, and nobody to give anyone help."

". . . just like you step in something, you just sink and you can't get out of it. You get in this place and, I don't know, there is something about it that just keeps you. I guess it's the low adequacy of the housing . . . the low morals of the whole place. It's one big nothing. It's one big nothing. I mean you can live here for millions and millions of years and you will see the same place, same time and same situation. It's just like time stops here."

[And in Boston, Massachusetts.]

"[A person] rents a brokendown room for $21 to $24 a week that is rat infested and has cockroaches running all over the place. There are holes in the ceiling where the plaster has fallen down and the people have to share a bathroom. The so-called furnished apartments usually contain a few chairs, a table, and an old rusty bed. . . . Frequently social workers tell families to move out of these homes where the rents are too high, but they never find them decent homes where rents are lower."

"In the section of Roxbury in which I live we have been fighting for street lights for quite some time. But they have completely ignored us. Our street is dark and though we have been writing letters and we have been getting some answers, nothing has happened. I feel it is because this area is predominantly Negro. If it was any other area, they would have gotten action."

"Police have isolated the South End as an area, giving it only token protection. Prostitution, bookmaking and after-hours places are all over and there is an excess of liquor stores and a shortage of foot patrolmen to keep the street safe. A hotel located near police headquarters, and known throughout the city as a house of prostitution, was closed by police after a Boston newspaper publicized it. But it opened again after about two months and is now back in business."

What Do You Think?

1. Some of the testimony hints at a sense of hopelessness that grows up in ghetto slum conditions. Is it possible that this sense of hopelessness could have an influence on continuing such conditions? Explain.

2.   The people who testified before the commission were mostly poor people. Do poor people have particular problems in getting a hearing for their grievances? Explain.

3.   The United States is the richest nation in the world. Even the poor here often have things that would be considered middle class in other parts of the world (a car, a television set, a telephone). Do poor people in America have problems that other poor people do not have? Is this a very difficult nation to live in if you are poor?

4. A CLOSE LOOK AT A GHETTO SLUM *

Kenneth Clark knows Harlem well. He has worked there and has seen what happens to people forced to live in ghetto conditions.

Another important aspect of the social dynamics of the Northern urban ghettos is the fact that all are crowded and poor; Harlem houses 232,792 people within its three and one-half square miles—a valley between Morningside and Washington Heights and the Harlem River. There are more than 100 people per acre. Ninety per cent of the 87,369 residential buildings are more than thirty-three years old, and nearly half were built before 1900. Private developers have not thought Harlem a good investment: Few of the newer buildings were sponsored by private money, and almost all of those buildings erected since 1929 are post-World War II public housing developments, where a fifth of the population lives.

The condition of all but the newest buildings is poor. Eleven per cent are classified as dilapidated by the 1960 census; that is, they do "not provide safe and adequate shelter," and thirty-three per cent are deteriorating (i.e. "need more repair than would be provided in the course of regular maintenance"). There are more people in fewer rooms than elsewhere in the city. Yet the rents and profits from Harlem are often high, as many landlords deliberately crowd more people into buildings in slum areas, knowing that the poor have few alternatives. The rent per room is often higher in Harlem than for better equipped buildings downtown. Slum landlords, ready enough when the rent is due, are hard to find when repairs are demanded. Even the city cannot seem to find some of them, and when they go to trial for neglect, they are usually given modest and lenient sentences—compared to the sentences of Harlem teenagers who defy the law. Cruel in the extreme is the landlord who,

---

* From "Housing Decay," in *Dark Ghetto,* by Kenneth B. Clark. Copyright © 1965 by Kenneth B. Clark. Reprinted by permission of Harper & Row, Publishers.

like the store owner who charges Negroes more for shoddy merchandise, exploits the powerlessness of the poor. For the poor are not only poor but unprotected and do not know how to seek redress. One is reminded of the Biblical admonition: "for whosoever hath, to him shall be given, and he shall have more abundance: but whosoever hath not, from him shall be taken away even that he hath."

In Harlem, a Haryou interviewer had a conversation with a little girl about her home that revealed both the apathy and the hope of the ghetto:

Interviewer: Tell me something about you—where were you born, you know, where you grew up, how everything went for you?

Gwen D.: When I was born I lived on 118th Street. There was a man killed in the hallway, and a man died right in front of the door where I lived at. My mother moved after that man got killed. I liked it in 97th Street because it was integration in that block. All kinds of people lived there.

Interviewer: Spanish people? White people?

Gwen D.: Spanish people, Italian people, all kinds of people. I liked it because it wasn't one group of whites and one group of Negroes or Spanish or something like that; everybody who lived in that block were friends.

Interviewer: How come you moved?

Gwen D.: Well, my mother she didn't like the building too well.

Interviewer: What didn't she like about it?

Gwen D.: Well, it was falling down.

Interviewer: In your whole life, has anything happened to you that you really got excited about?

Gwen D.: I can't remember.

Interviewer: Tell me about some real good times you've had in your life.

Gwen D.: In Harlem?

Interviewer: In your life, that you've really enjoyed.

Gwen D.: One year we was in summer school and we went to this other school way downtown, out of Harlem, to give a show and everybody was so happy. And we were on television, and I saw myself, and I was the only one with a clean skirt and blouse.

Interviewer: What kind of changes would you want to make? Changes so that you can have a better chance, your sisters can have a better chance, and your brother?

Gwen D.: Well, I just want a chance to do what I can.

*   *   *   *   *

About one out of every seven or eight adults in Harlem is unemployed. In the city as a whole the rate of unemployment is half that. Harlem is a young community, compared to the rest of New York, and in 1960 twice as many young Negro men in the labor force, as compared to their white counterparts, were without jobs. For the girls, the gap was even greater—nearly two and one-half times the unemployment rate for white girls in the labor force. Across the country the picture is very much the same. Unemployment of Negroes is rising much faster than unemployment of whites. Among young men eighteen to twenty-four, the national rate is five times as high for Negroes as for whites.

An optimist could point to the fact that the average family income of Negroes has increased significantly within the two decades 1940–1960, but a more realistic observer would have to qualify this with the fact that the *discrepancy* between the average family income of whites and that of Negroes has increased even more significantly. The real income, the relative status income, of Negroes has gone down during a period when the race was supposed to have been making what candidates for elective office call "the most dramatic progress of any oppressed group at any period of human history."

The menial and unrewarding jobs available to most Negroes can only mean a marginal subsistence for most ghetto families: the median income in Harlem is $3,480 compared to $5,103 for residents of New York City—a similar gap exists in the country as a whole. Half of the families in Harlem have incomes under $4,000, while 75 per cent of all New York City residents earn more than $4,000. Only one in twenty-five Negro families has an income above $10,000, while more than four in twenty-five of the white families do.

Nor do Negroes with an education receive the financial benefits available to whites. Herman P. Miller in his book, *Rich Man, Poor Man,* states that Negroes who have completed four years of college *"can expect to earn only as much in a lifetime as whites who have not gone beyond the eighth grade."* This is true both in the North and in the South. The white high school graduate will earn just about as much as a Negro who has gone through college and beyond for graduate training. One young man in Harlem asked: "What is integration into poverty?" The question is not easy to answer.

Both the men and the women in the ghetto are relegated to the lowest status jobs. Sixty-four per cent of the men in Harlem compared to only 39 per cent of New York City's male population, and 74 per cent of the women compared to 37 per cent for New York City, hold unskilled and service jobs. Only 7 per cent of Harlem males are professionals, technicians, managers, proprietors, or officials. Twenty-four per cent of the males in the city hold such prestige posts.

An eighteen-year-old Negro boy protested: "They keep telling us about job opportunities, this job opportunity, and that, but who wants a job working all week and bringing home a sweat man's pay?" Most of the men in the dark ghetto do work for a "sweat man's pay," and even *that* is now threatened by the rise of automation.

---

1. What is your reaction to the interview presented? Ask and answer the same questions of yourself. Compare your answers with Gwen's.
2. Clark thinks employment has something to do with slum conditions. What connection do you see, if any? Explain.

5.   BAD HOUSING = SOCIAL ILLS? *

Bad housing has been blamed for many social ills. The National Advisory Commission on Civil Disorders included a chapter on housing in its report on the disorders that convulsed American cities in the sixties. The charts below illustrate some of the Commission's findings. What do these charts reveal as to the quality of white and black housing in the United States?

In 14 of the largest U. S. cities, the proportions of all nonwhite housing units classified as deteriorating, dilapidated, or lacking full plumbing in 1960 (the latest data for which figures are available), were as follows:

City	Percentage of Nonwhite Occupied Housing Units Classified Deteriorating or Dilapidated, 1960	Percentage of Nonwhite Occupied Housing Units Classified Deteriorating, Dilapidated, or Sound but Without Full Plumbing, 1960
New York	33.8	42.4
Chicago	32.1	42.8
Los Angeles	14.7	18.1
Philadelphia	28.6	32.0
Detroit	27.9	30.1
Baltimore	30.5	31.7
Houston	30.1	36.7

---

* Excerpted from the *Report of the National Advisory Commission on Civil Disorders,* United States Riot Commission, March 1, 1968.

City	Percentage of Non-white Occupied Housing Units Classified Deteriorating or Dilapidated, 1960	Percentage of Non-white Occupied Housing Units Classified Deteriorating, Dilapidated, or Sound but Without Full Plumbing, 1960
Cleveland	29.9	33.9
Washington, D. C.	15.2	20.8
St. Louis	40.3	51.6
San Francisco	21.3	34.0
Dallas	41.3	45.9
New Orleans	44.3	56.9
Pittsburgh	49.1	58.9

Source: U. S. Department of Commerce, Bureau of the Census

The commission carried out special analyses of 1960 housing conditions in three cities, concentrating on all Census Tracts with 1960 median incomes of under $3,000 for both families and individuals. It also analyzed housing conditions in Watts. Do the results indicate any relationship between race and poor housing?

Item	Detroit	Washington, D. C.	Memphis	Watts Area of Los Angeles
Total population of study area	162,375	97,094	150,827	49,074
Percentage of study area nonwhite	67.5	74.5	74.0	87.3
Percentage of Housing Units in study area: —Substandard by HUD definition	32.7	23.9	35.0	10.5
—Dilapidated, deteriorating or sound but lacking full plumbing	53.1	37.3	46.5	29.1

Source: U. S. Department of Commerce, Bureau of the Census

"The combination of high rents and low incomes forces many Negroes to pay an excessively high proportion of their income on housing." Does the following chart, showing the percentage of renter households paying over 35 per cent of their incomes for rent in ten metropolitan areas, support or refute this statement?

Percentages of White and Nonwhite Occupied Units with Households Paying 35 Per cent or More of Their Income For Rent in Selected Metropolitan Areas

Metropolitan Area	White Occupied Units	Nonwhite Occupied Units
Cleveland	8.6	33.8
Dallas	19.2	33.8
Detroit	21.2	40.5
Kansas City	20.2	40.0
Los Angeles-Long Beach	23.4	28.4
New Orleans	16.6	30.5
Philadelphia	19.3	32.1
Saint Louis	18.5	36.7
San Francisco-Oakland	21.2	25.1
Washington, D. C.	18.5	28.3

Source: U. S. Department of Commerce, Bureau of the Census

What Do You Think?

1. Look carefully at the three charts. Which group lives under the worst conditions? Which group pays the most for its living space? What would happen to these prices if there were housing alternatives available? Explain.

2. It has been argued that by raising the income levels of black families through a guaranteed annual wage or some other device, it would be possible for such families to obtain adequate housing. What is your opinion on this matter? State your reasons.

6.   OPEN HOUSING: CIVIL RIGHT OR CIVIC FRIGHT? *

What are the results of discriminatory housing? Here are two opposing views.

Civil Right!

Discrimination in Housing Violates Negroes' Constitutional Rights

"The freedom of white property owners to discriminate in the sale of their houses denies to millions of minority group homeseekers the freedom to purchase the property of their choice." So said the *Christian Century* magazine in a recent editorial on open housing.

The results of discriminatory practices in housing are truly appalling. According to testimony given by Urban League Director Whitney Young to the judiciary subcommittee of the House of Representatives, 80 per cent of the Negroes in Washington, D. C., and 71.6 per cent of those in Newark, N. J., live in segregated housing. "The facts show," said Young, "that the Negro has not been permitted to disperse . . . For the Negro, the port of entry in the central cities has become a prison."

This segregation is not only unfair, it is also unconstitutional. The 14th Amendment to the U. S. Constitution guarantees "equal protection of the laws" to all U. S. citizens. For the Negro homeseeker, the guarantee is little more than a hollow mockery.

Isn't it high time that Congress made it possible for *all* U. S. Citizens to enjoy *all* Constitutional guarantees? As Representative Jeffrey Cohelan (D., Calif.) puts it: "One of the traditional rights of an American is that of freely selecting a place to live subject only to what his means permit. The freedom is so basic and so widespread among most of us that it is taken for granted. But this freedom does not exist for Negroes."

Open Housing Legislation Would Not Hurt White Houseowners

"I believe it is accurate to say that individual homeowners do not control the pattern of housing in communities of any size. The main components of the housing industry are builders, landlords, real estate brokers, and those who provide mortgage money. These are the groups which maintain housing patterns based on race." Thus did former U. S. Attorney General Nicholas Katzenbach pinpoint one of the most significant factors behind segregated housing.

---

* Reprinted by permission from *Senior Scholastic,* © 1968 by Scholastic Magazines, Inc.

Katzenbach went on to point out that it isn't necessarily racial bias that causes these groups to discriminate. Such discrimination is more often a reflection of the "misconception that neighborhoods must remain racially separate to maintain real estate values." In fact, government studies over the past 10 years show that the opposite is true. Real estate values in racially mixed neighborhoods have generally remained stable or increased in value.

Despite all the "scare tactics" used against it, open housing legislation will not destroy neighborhoods. On the contrary, it may ease community tensions by giving Negroes and whites the opportunity to associate with one another and make friendships that will end the destructive antagonisms now existing.

Ghetto Housing Is at the Root of Many of the Negro's Problems

"Why be a lawyer, or a doctor, or a dentist, or a successful business-man, if you cannot use the money you make to live in the house in which you want to live? What good is it to work night and day to achieve success if you cannot provide your family with a decent home?" Thus did Representative William T. Cahill (R., N. J.,) sum up one of the most perplexing problems facing Negroes in the U. S. today: What's the point of struggling to get ahead if the money you earn won't buy you the things a white man can buy?

There's little doubt in the minds of most experts that inadequate housing has been a major factor in limiting the progress made by individual Negroes to date. As Representative Cohelan puts it: "The discriminatory practices which confine (Negroes) to the slums of the central city work at the same time to bind them to poor schools and to a generally unhealthy environment. There are ample independent studies to document that bad housing breeds bad health and to connect deprived living conditions with low educational motivation."

One thing is certain: the discriminatory practices that have confined Negroes to a ghetto existence aren't going to go away by themselves. Congress has a moral responsibility to rip down the wall of bigotry that for so long has consigned Negroes to a second-class status in their own country.

Civic Fright!

Individuals Have the Right to Sell Their Homes to Whom They Please

"No State shall make or enforce any law which shall abridge the privileges or immunities of citizens of the United States; nor shall any State deprive any citizen of life, liberty, or *property* without due process of law; nor deny to any person within its jurisdiction the equal protection of the laws." This portion of the 14th Amendment to the U. S. Constitution indicates that open housing legislation now before Congress would violate the rights of U. S. citizens by *requiring* property owners to sell to people they may not want to sell to.

The legislation would thus, in effect, mean that the homes of U. S. citizens would no longer belong exclusively to them. As Representative William M. Tuck (D., Va.) has put it: "No one can consider himself the owner of property if the government has the right to dictate to him the terms of its disposal."

Actually, the notion that one man has the "right" to buy any home he pleases is mistaken because it means that another man has a "duty" to sell him his home—whether he wants to or not. The U. S. Constitution clearly protects property rights. Open housing legislation just as clearly violates that protection.

Open Housing Will Not Solve Civil Rights Problems

Supporters of open housing claim that it's a necessary step to give Negroes meaningful equality with whites. But equally meaningful is the matter of Negro responsibility. After last summer's destructive riots, and the property damage involved, many whites question what will happen if Negroes move into white residential neighborhoods. Many whites have made enormous sacrifices to buy their homes and keep up their property. If Negroes move in next door and property values plummet, many whites fear that their lifetime savings may disappear.

To date, little has been done to attack the real problems barring the Negro from making real progress. The single greatest deterrent to progress in civil rights—economic advancement for the Negro—is totally ignored in the arguments over open housing. According to Representative John B. Anderson (R., Ill.), a Negro leader in Chicago told him that only about two per cent of Chicago's 812,000 Negroes would be affected by a federal open housing law. The rest wouldn't be helped at all since they don't have the money to buy or rent better housing anyway. One sociologist points out that only about three per cent of U. S. Negroes earn more than $7,000 a year, which is close to the minimum needed to buy a home in the suburbs, according to U. S. government statistics.

In fact, the only probable effect the new law would have on these Negroes would be to increase their dissatisfaction as soon as they learn that the new law isn't the cure-all its supporters claim it to be.

Open Housing Legislation Will Lead to Unwarranted
Intrusions by Government into the Private Sector

"Those who clamor so loudly for federal action to correct what they regard as a wrong should reflect that this same federal action may some day be used against them." Thus did Representative Armistead I. Selden,

Jr. (D., Alabama), sum up the fears of many regarding open housing laws.

The fear that the new law may lead to government intervention in the private affairs of U. S. citizens is well founded. Rarely has the federal tendency to do so been so clear as it is in the case of open housing. All of the provisions are weighted in favor of the complainant, so much so that just about the only right the homeowner receives is the right to defend himself in court at his own expense—while the government picks up the tab for his accuser.

As Representative Joe D. Waggonner, Jr. (D., La.), puts it: "Where there are no property rights there are no human rights. The right to own and hold to oneself the product of your labor and sweat is the very seedbed of democracy. Without this seedbed, there is no place for human rights to grow and flourish."

What Do You Think?

1. Those who argue for open housing legislation claim that it is imperative if we are to break down the barriers which divide blacks and whites in this country. Do you agree? Why? or why not?
2. Property rights are indispensable for human rights, say those who oppose open housing. Define property rights and human rights. Is the statement true? Why?

7. WHAT PRICE DO WE PAY FOR OUR SLUMS? *

A major cost brought about by slum conditions is welfare. All across the country, welfare payments have increased. What problems does welfare bring to our cities? What alternatives to welfare might exist?

The largest single item in [New York's] new budget is also the unhappiest, both for the taxpayer on the giving end and those who benefit from it: welfare.

In the fiscal year [1968] that starts July 1, the Human Resources Administration is asking for nearly $1.4 billion to help an ever-expanding army of men, women, and children to exist at a standard lower than the federal government regards as minimal.

---

* From George H. Favre, "Rising Welfare Costs Tackled," January 16, 1968. Reprinted by permission from *The Christian Science Monitor.* © 1968 The Christian Science Monitor Publishing Society.

For the first time in this city's history—and, it is believed, in the history of any city—welfare costs will exceed that of running the public-school system.

The new budget submitted by Mitchell I. Ginsberg, human-resources administrator, is a whopping 51 per cent higher than the $918 million allowed for fiscal year 1966–67. But last year's budget allowance fell far short of the $1.071 billion actually spent.

Behind the soaring costs is the steady addition of some 14,000 new names to the welfare rolls each month. There were 780,000 on the city's dole at the end of 1967. By this time next year the figures will be around a million. That is one out of every eight persons living in the city.

REASONS FOR RAPID RISE

Mr. Ginsberg gives several reasons for the rapid rise in welfare numbers. Among them: a continuing inflow of poor persons from rural areas, particularly the South and Puerto Rico; a continued trickle out of the city of white middle-class families; continued decline of manufacturing jobs; few jobs for the unskilled; attrition of even those remaining jobs by automation; and a wider awareness among poor people who have not been on welfare that they are eligible for aid.

On this last count, the activities of civil-rights leaders and organization of the poor are alerting many who did not know they were eligible.

But if New York is the first city to see welfare costs exceed public school spending, it is hardly the only city with a growing welfare problem. Nor is it the worst off, in terms of how sharply the welfare cost curve slants upward.

Mr. Ginsberg says St. Louis, Buffalo, Newark, and most of the suburbs surrounding New York are having even sharper increases than his own city.

Welfare is not a static affair, either in the numbers of persons affected or in how long they are dependent on aid.

In 1967, for example, some 99,000 persons moved off the city's welfare rolls. But another 161,000 new cases were added. Of these, 34,000 came on because of jobs lost. Another 31,000 suffered incapacitating illness; 27,000 were eligible because of inadequate earnings; 19,000 were women and children whose husbands and fathers had deserted them; 50,000 were for other reasons.

LINDSAY PRESENTS FIGURES

Last fall, in testimony before Congress, Mayor John V. Lindsay told the House Ways and Means Committee that 79 per cent of all welfare recipients in New York City are children and adults caring for them; 15 per cent cannot support themselves because of age or disability; and only 2,600 men on welfare had a usable skill to qualify for a job without considerable training and rehabilitation.

These figures for New York City appear to contradict the often-expressed criticism that welfare recipients are lazy ne'er-do-wells who would rather live on the public dole than work.

National statistics indicate the same. Robert H. Jugge, head of the Bureau of Family Services in the United States Department of Health, Education, and Welfare, says that in 1966 only 56,000 "unemployed but employable fathers" were on welfare across the nation, out of more than 8 million recipients.

SPENDING COMPARED

The total also included 110,000 incapacitated fathers; 900,000 mothers, most of whose husbands had divorced or deserted them; 2 million persons 65 years or older; 500,000 permanently disabled; 85,000 blind; and 3.5 million children.

Nationally, the annual cost of welfare runs around $6.5 billion, of which $3.5 billion is paid by the federal government and $3 billion is paid from state and local tax receipts.

Daniel P. Moynihan, noted authority on urban problems, says that this expenditure is "quite low" compared to other Western nations.

Welfare spending in the United States in recent years has run consistently at around 1 per cent of personal income. In New York State, in 1965, the figure was 0.97 per cent of personal income.

But if the national welfare cost is low relative to other countries, it is a staggering burden to major metropolitan cities like New York. Even with the federal and state governments picking up 70 per cent of the tab, New York City is left with a difference of more than $400 million.

In hopes of cutting this back, Mr. Ginsberg has recommended that the state pick up medicaid costs. Out of the $1.4 billion welfare total, $300 million is earmarked for medicaid, up $100 million over last year's budget.

On another front, Mr. Ginsberg is experimenting with some novel ways of cutting back the actual numbers of welfare recipients. His most recent proposal is an effort to get industry to pledge itself to set aside 5 per cent of all jobs that open up for welfare recipients. This proposal has a counterpart in Great Britain, where a law has been passed requiring employers to keep 3 per cent of their jobs open for handicapped persons.

Welfare Rolls—New York's Newest Applicants
1967: 161,000 new appeals for welfare filed for the reasons shown.

Deserted by husbands or fathers (19,000)	Incapacitated by illness (31,000)
	Lost jobs (34,000)
Returned from institutions (25,000)	Miscellaneous (new births, etc.)
Inadequate earnings (27,000)	(25,000)

What Do You Think?

1.   In looking at the chart above, which of the categories listed furnished the most new applicants for welfare? Which one furnished the least? Are there any explanations for this?
2.   Looking at the categories presented, where could cuts be made? As mayor of a major city, would you move to cut welfare costs? Why? Are there any alternatives to welfare? What are they?
3.   Some people claim that the best way to lower welfare costs is to put all the recipients back to work. Do you think this is a possible solution? Explain.

8.   CONGRESS TAKES STEPS *

The need for housing in the nation has been recognized in the Congress. A new bill paves the way for "1.7 million new or renovated housing units in the next three years" (through 1972). Here are some of its provisions.

· *The home-ownership plan,* for families with income ranging from $3,000 to $8,000, would enable purchases of a home for as little as $200 down and a monthly payment equal to 20 per cent of the family's gross income. The government would provide anything over that figure in payments for principle, interest, tax and mortgage insurance. Families would be allowed to buy homes priced up to $15,000 in most states, and up to $20,000 in certain high-cost areas. The plan's cost during the first year is pegged at $75 million, eventually rising to $300 million after three years. Expected yield: 500,000 housing units, including single family homes and condominiums.

· *Rent subsidy programs* would be expanded from $40 million in 1969 to $100 million in 1970. Families would be required to pay 25 per cent of incomes for rent—an amount that some consider unduly stiff. But the biggest boon is probably in a mortgage-interest rates subsidy for organizations that will provide new or renovated rental apartment units for low- or middle-income families. In a manner similar to the home-ownership plan, the government would subsidize all but one percentage point of such an interest charge. The cost is estimated at $300 million over three years to build or renovate 700,000 housing units.

---

* Excerpted from "Housing's Marshall Plan," *Newsweek,* August 5, 1968.

So far, very good—and reviewing the omnibus bill, HUD's Wood [former Under Secretary Robert C. Wood] said it represented a real "determination to come to grips with the housing problems of the very poor." Yet Congress's determination was visibly wavering in the icy blasts of the current economy drive. "It's easy to pass an authorization," said one skeptical official. "Appropriations could be the real test."

The cost of the bill may not be as high as its $5.4 billion label. Because much of the money is to be loaned or put up as guarantees, repayments should hold the cost to an average $300 million a year for the next ten years. Even so, HUD's regular appropriation for the current fiscal year is still being debated, and the agency will probably have to seek a supplemental bill from a penny-pinching Congress in September to pay for the new programs. Beyond that, HUD's own payroll is supposed to be slashed along with other governmental agencies to the levels of June, 1966, making it hard to administer any new efforts.

Yet for all their real misgivings, HUD officials saw some reasons for encouragement. For one thing, they pointed out, many of the same congressmen who had voted for spending cuts also voted for the housing bill—which might indicate that they wanted the cuts made elsewhere. And failing all else, the bill does authorize action for fully three years. Sometime during that span a Senate aide said hopefully last week, "things could ease up."

What Do You Think?

1. Congress can provide the money but this will not do the job alone. Check the next two readings and see what advances are being made in science and technology which will also help create housing. How do these new advances relate to the bill passed by Congress?

2. How will this bill benefit the people living in the central city ghettos of America? How will workers and corporations benefit? How will you benefit?

9.   DO TECHNOLOGY AND MONEY OFFER HOPE?

The next two articles deal with the possibilities provided by science and technology.

Low-Priced Homes? *

Can we build a better house cheaper? Former President Lyndon Johnson believes we can.

[Former] President Johnson envisioned . . . an industrial breakthrough that will bring the cost of attractive, comfortable, well-built homes down as low as $5000. . . .

Robert Weaver [former Secretary of Housing and Urban Development] armed the President with figures.

If a house can be erected here costing $5500 at the current 6¾ per cent FHA insured interest rate, then, Johnson said, under the new housing bill's "home ownership" interest subsidy plan:

· The monthly charge would be $48 including principle, interest, taxes, and insurance.

· This means a family of two earning about $1700 a year could buy the house paying $28 a month, with the government paying $20.

If the home costs $7500, Weaver told the President, the monthly charge would be $67 and "a family of four with two young children earning $3000 a year will be able to own the home by paying $39 monthly with the government paying $28."

The chief executive also said he is directing Weaver to "take every step necessary to promote the exchange of information and housing technology with other nations."

Is More Money The Answer? *

What are some obstacles to reducing the cost of new urban housing?

Excuses for the high cost of replacing the housing in the core and nearby sections of cities are plentiful . . . [T]he ridges in the money mountains between the people living in slums and the kind of housing they aspire to are high—but not necessarily impassable.

---

* Excerpted from Sydney Kossen, "LBJ—Kaiser Housing Plan," *San Francisco Examiner,* August 11, 1968.
* Excerpted from *Science and the City,* U. S. Department of Housing and Urban Development.

Three of the most conspicuous obstacles to reducing the cost of new urban housing are:

1. The scarcity of land. Absentee owners, disputing heirs, and speculators profit from holding sites on which many people would like to live.

2. Costly constraints. Legal and financial requirements serve as treaties between vested interests to preserve the status quo.

3. The construction industry. Its fragmented structure has kept it from fighting costs with new methods and machinery as fiercely as, say, the auto or the chemical industries.

To venturesome engineers the scarcity of land looks like a figment of tired old men's imaginations. Reinforced concrete, stronger metallic girders, and new construction techniques are increasing the use of building sites on top of one another. New housing now can be built above almost anything, including old housing. Much more might be done if we tackled the density-of-people problem in the same logical and determined way that we have tackled the density-of-the-atmosphere problem to explore space.

To impartial observers, many city governments appear to have let their power to tax rust. If tax pressures were used to make it more advantageous to holders of slum lots to put them to better use, most owners would do it or sell them to invest elsewhere. Although some cities are giving tax concessions to landowners for improving structures, in most cities an heir's taxes go up if he modernizes a building that someone left to him.

Violations of housing laws now fatten some slum landlords' billfolds. These laws would be enforced better if there were more neighborhood welfare centers to which tenants could go for information and legal advice. Better enforcement of occupancy laws could reduce the cost to the whole city of health, sanitation, and other services.

Updating building codes would remove constraints that prevent economies in construction. By specifying the materials and methods that builders must use, old codes prevent innovations such as plastic piping and new structural components.

To conquer space and atoms, engineers have devised testing systems by which the reliability and lifetime of nearly anything that a factory can produce can be predicted. Automatic nondestructive testing equipment is becoming less expensive. Its use is making it feasible to substitute performance requirements and reliability tests for materials specifications. Why should anyone invent a component or invest in an innovation in housing that he must fight city hall for permission to exploit? Codes are written to safeguard people, but this does not require that they discourage progress. Many clauses of many codes could be safely rewritten in ways to save people money.

Government has removed many boulders from the road to lower-cost housing, but has scarcely touched others. Why should it cost more and take longer to transfer title to a machine that stays put, such as a building, than to one that can be driven wherever one wants to take it? Both legal and financial customs are factors in the cost of housing. Must we go on forever doing the same old things in the same old ways?

The construction industry's structure has retarded its progress. Small companies produce most of America's housing. Their size limits their credit resources, they must often lay off their workers, they cannot afford costly research and experiments, and they learn too slowly about changes in the state of the building art. Macy's knows in minutes what Gimbel's does to reduce prices, but it takes a long time for tens of thousands of builders scattered across a continent to look over each other's shoulders.

Such simple devices as plastic sheeting to keep the rain off workers have lessened the constraints that weather places on builders. Economists have suggested that large companies could afford the research necessary to bring about more such innovations. Large companies might also stabilize their employees' incomes to a greater extent than small concerns can. Possibly they could persuade investors and city governments to remove antique constraints on the construction of homes more quickly too.

Men's fear of change is a basic reason for the high cost of urban housing. Fear of the future underlies the craftsman's opposition to mechanization, his hesitancy to admit newcomers to his union, and jurisdictional disputes between unions. The age of some of our laws and the conservatism of investors amplify this fear. Some of it is the result of forgetfulness and misinterpretations of history's lessons.

Men will gladly risk a trip to the moon because researchers have measured the hazards, and engineers have built a long roster of reliable devices to reduce them. Anthropologists and financiers and statesmen could work together with other specialists to survey the hazards of urban life similarly. Then ways might be found to minimize many of them.

What Do You Think?

1. The newspaper story indicated that a prospective homeowner's primary concern is with money. Why should he be so concerned about interest rates and monthly charges? From your previous readings, what do you know about the cost of housing?

2. "Men fear change," say the authors of the second article. Do you? What kinds of change are most threatening to people? What kinds are least threatening? Explain.

3. The authors of *Science and the City* make a case for increased use of automatic testing equipment to predict performance of

products. From what you have heard or read about computers, what do you feel about greater use of them throughout the society? Are there any dangers involved in the use of computers? What are they?

10.   CAN PEOPLE ESCAPE TO THE SUBURBS? *

For many who have moved from the central city, the answer to their housing needs has been the suburban bungalow. The areas around our cities have grown fantastically and are continuing to grow. But problems exist there, too.

As the critics see it, suburbia looks something like this: every tree in the neighborhood has been bulldozed to make way for marching rows of absolutely identical little houses. In them live the world's most rigid conformists, who anxiously ape every mannerism or material purchase made by the family in the next house. Everybody acts just like everybody else—and if one individual or family violates the norm, they are ostracized. Beneath it the suburbanites are all bored to tears. Yet they engage in a frantic round of visiting and barbecuing and cocktailing to keep up on the gossip. The men leave to work in the city at about 6:30 A.M. and get home at 7:30 P.M. after the younger children are in bed. Mom runs everything since nobody sees Dad except on weekends—when Saturdays are devoted to the war against weeds, crab-grass, and peeling paint, and Sundays are reserved for golf. The children are basically mother-dominated brats. The teenagers, though often spoiled, are mercilessly harassed by their social-climbing parents to get into Princeton or Smith, or some other prestigious college which will help assure that they, too, "make good."

This—and much more—has become the present day image of that never-never land called suburbia. It is an image that absolutely horrifies most architects, social planners, city planners, sociologists, and critical journalists. Yet, as it happens, they are the ones most responsible for popularizing the image of conformity and sterility in the suburbs.

The trouble with the image is that while it contains a large fragment of truth and insight into the very real problems of the suburbs, it really doesn't jibe with the actual place where millions of Americans happen to live—which is suburbia. Most suburbanites like it there. They find it healthier, more attractive, and more comfortable than where they lived before. They are, in fact, making the suburbs the most popular place to live in America. For, while the image of suburbia has suffered

---

* "What's Wrong (and Right) with Our Suburbs?" Reprinted by permission from *Senior Scholastic*, © 1968 by Scholastic Magazines, Inc.

from the brickbats of the critics, the home-buying public has made suburbia itself a sellout success. Unswayed by the uncomplimentary portraits, the public has been happily flinging itself into the suburbs at an accelerating rate for decades. In recent years, suburbs have grown about five times faster than the central cities they ring.

It is often said that 70 per cent of all Americans now live in "urban areas." But the U. S. Census Bureau describes any place with more than 2,500 people as an "urban area." The fact is that most of that urban 70 per cent live in places with populations under 50,000 in small towns or in suburbs. It becomes increasingly clear with each census that we have become a more suburban nation than an urban nation.

What is happening is a continuation of an old, old story in the U. S. As people are drawn off the farms and away from the rural areas, they head first for the central cities where the jobs are. If they are economically successful, they (or the next generation of their family) move on out to the suburbs "for the children." As they usually explain it, the move is made because they feel cramped in the city. Their apartment isn't big enough. They want separate bedrooms for the children, a private yard for the kids to play in, a place to park the car. Also, they want to own their home, not pay rent.

A few years ago, Raymond Vernon, a Harvard Business School economist, began conducting one of the most thorough studies of a metropolitan area yet made. As he went along, Vernon says, he began wondering why the general public tended to disregard all the critical commentary about the suburbs. The answer, as he sees it, is that to most Americans the suburbs represent progress and improvement. "They see their lot as being better than that of their parents and confidently expect their children to do a little better," says Vernon. Thus, while critics have pinpointed the flaws and problems that have developed in the headlong suburbanization of America, the general public has been more concerned with the personal benefits it has brought—and therefore has minimized the importance of what the critics have been saying. Yet the problems the critics talk about have been growing and growing—so much so that fewer and fewer suburbanites are minimizing them anymore. To mention just some of the more pressing:

• Services often have not kept pace with population. As population has multiplied—a hundredfold in some areas—existing governments have been unable to provide the needed (or expected) services quickly. Sewer lines have to be laid, schools opened and staffed, libraries built, police and fire departments increased or even organized from scratch. These things take time and money. To pay for this array of services, the suburbs have been boosting taxes—primarily property taxes. Since many people choose their particular suburb partly on the basis of its reputation for "low taxes," they are outraged when those taxes start climbing skyward. Some taxes have been climbing at a clip that has led to taxpayers' revolts. The schools have been prime victims of these revolts—for school taxes and school budgets are often the only specific tax item a citizen can actually vote against. For example, in New York's Nassau County (one of the richest counties in the U. S.), voters in the various school districts rejected 25 of 56 school budgets last May. When taxes are then voted down or school budgets slashed, other citizens step up the volume of complaints about deficiencies in the schools or in other local services. It can be a vicious circle.

· Professional criminals are being increasingly drawn to suburbia by its affluence. Two years ago, the FBI startled many people by announcing that the crime rate had increased six times faster in the suburbs than in America's central cities. Moreover, more than half of all serious crime in the suburbs is committed by teenagers 18 and under, says the FBI. Local officials are more alarmed, however, at the influx of professional burglars and organized criminals into affluent suburbs. Most suburban police departments have neither the manpower, the facilities, nor the training to deal with an influx of professional criminals.

· Many suburban areas lack workable municipal governments to run them. Systems of government that worked fine when the population was a stable 3,000 creak and groan under the strain of trying to service 90,000. Often, too, jurisdictions overlap. A single family may live under several single-groove governments—a fire district with one set of boundaries, a school district with another, a library district with another, a sanitation district with yet another.

· Although there are exceptions, most suburbs are virtually all-white. Many have formal or informal agreements that keep nonwhites from buying homes. When Negroes appear to look at a house with a "for sale" sign, they are usually told that it is no longer available. Despite a number of state and local laws to prevent such discrimination in the sale of housing, some sociologists believe that a situation is developing in many areas where cities will become predominantly Negro and suburbs will be white. Such a cleavage—if it develops—could have serious (some would say disastrous) repercussions in American life.

Until recently it was possible to talk about a town or a city or a suburb. But the U. S. is changing, and increasingly the urban landscape is overlapping itself. Several years ago the French geographer Jean Gottmann led a pioneering study of the U. S. eastern seaboard from Boston to Virginia. He found it to be a near-continuous strip of urban development. He called it megalopolis and said it was the pattern of the future for many parts of the U. S. (Southern California, for instance) and eventually the world.

Many people have misunderstood megalopolis to mean one great big super city—thickly populated and highly industrialized. It does not mean that. It is instead a pathwork of urban development—here thick, there thin, a conglomeration of city, suburb, exurb (even farther away from the city than suburb), and any other urb someone someday might invent. Megalopolis encloses several large cities and hundreds of small towns, villages, and communities. Each new community on the fringe of an existing urban center helps to fill in the still green spaces of megalopolis and to further melt the different parts of the urban conglomerate together.

From this viewpoint, the whole traditional dialogue about city vs suburb may soon be outmoded. In the heavily urbanized areas a whole new kind of community—neither city nor country—is coming into being. This community is flung out along the roads. It is linked by the highways and made possible by those highways. It is diffused, unplanned, and to the trained eye of architects and planners, a chaotic and wasteful way to use land.

And more of the same seems to be on the way. By the year 2000 —just 32 years from now—the number of Americans living in and around cities is expected to double. Where will the houses and apartments to accommodate them be built? If the past and present are any guide, the answer is suburbia.

And here, really, lies suburbia's root problem today. Like Topsy, it "just growed"—often too fast. Nobody bothered to figure out where would be the best and wisest places to locate industry, and where to save land for housing, and where parks would be needed, and where garbage could be dumped. Mostly the building up of the suburbs has occurred where farmers would sell their land. Sometimes the results were excellent. Sometimes they were a disaster.

Because of the proliferation and general weakness of local and county governments, usually no single authority had (or has) jurisdiction to guide such building in the public interest. Furthermore, the establishment of a single guiding authority is not in the American tradition. "Planning" to many Americans, smacks of centralized control of people's lives. So all the products of "no-planning" litter the landscape. Result: Suburban sprawl.

A British critic wrote recently that the roots of the sprawl problem go back to the roots of America. Says Ian Nairn of the London Observer: "Americans tend to forget that the pioneering era ended almost a century ago when the railways reached California. Land is still treated as though it were an expendable commodity like the buffalo. 'There'll always be more around the corner' is still the ruling principle." Nairn calls megalopolis a "disintegrating landscape," an environment of "total confusion and mediocrity," a place where you can drive for "hundreds of miles in what is supposed to be rural America without ever feeling really free of the suburban tentacles."

What depresses observers like Nairn is that it is not population growth alone that has scattered people over the suburban landscape. He points out that in European terms, the U. S. has no population problem at all. If the U. S. had the same population density as England and Wales, the whole U. S. population "could comfortably be fitted into Texas." Yet in England it is possible to leave a city and drive within a short period of time into what is clearly country—and very beautiful countryside at that.

What was done in England (and in some other European countries) has never been seriously attempted in the U. S. The Europeans have made national decisions on land use. They have planned ahead where housing would be built and where it would not be built. In England, a "green belt" around London was legislated. Here would be a stretch of open space that would serve several purposes: to protect farmlands close to city markets, and to give city dwellers "breathing room" and recreation sites. To help relieve the population pressure on London and other cities, Britain began building so-called "new towns" elsewhere.

Only in the past few years—and then in the hands of private builders with virtually no help from the government—has the idea of "new towns" been tried in the U. S. Nevertheless, it holds some bright promises for improving the liveability of at least some of the landscape of megalopolis.

We began this journey to suburbia with a look at the myths which surround it. As we have seen, the mythology neglects some of the far more real problems of suburbia and the metropolitan areas. By concentrating on such things as conformity (and several recent studies have shown the suburbanites don't conform any more or less than people living elsewhere), far more real problems of providing adequate services have tended to be overlooked.

Consider again the statement that between now and the year 2000 —a period of only 32 years—the number of Americans in or near cities will double. The implications are simply enormous when you imagine the homes and apartments, the schools and the roads, the sewers and the water mains that will be needed.

"If the present trends continue, those millions of new houses will inundate the countryside with sprawling, chaotic settlements on a scale dwarfing anything seen up to now," writes Edmund K. Faltermayer in Fortune. Faltermayer isn't one of the critics who complain about suburbs because they personally prefer living in the cities. He doesn't predict that we'll soon have no more land to stand on. "The danger," he says, "is rather that the country's metropolitan complexes will become so spread out as to destroy their liveability."

How much congestion, how much pollution, how many highway interchanges, how much sheer ugliness can a place develop before it simply becomes unfit for human habitation? In the past, we haven't asked these questions often enough, or insistently enough. Now, with suburbia upon us and in front of us, we are beginning to come up with some new answers.

The one point most of the critics can agree on is that some ways should be found to preserve open space close by the cities and suburbs —space where boys can play ball without being in someone's yard, where a family can picnic without driving for three hours to get there. Precisely how this should be done is open to heated debate—since it runs head on into a traditional American notion that the best thing to do with a piece of land is to make a buck on it—and as quickly as possible.

Under the present system, the pressure to sell land that is in the path of developers is almost irresistible. As housing developments near, taxes tend to rise. For a farmer, they can often rise so high—because his land is now more "valuable"—that he literally has to sell to the subdividers. One more piece of open land is now plowed up.

Some critics tend to argue for green "buffer" zones between cities —some of it in park land, some in farm land. Others suggest a less elaborate solution, one which is gaining favor among many developers: use of cluster zoning. Under this system, instead of laying out houses on a grid system, each with a big yard, houses are "clustered" closer together on looping roads. The amount of land saved by the shorter distance between houses and shorter roads is then used for "community land." It is open space used by the entire community in much the same way the old "village green" or "village common" in New England towns belonged to everyone.

Basically, however, what the critics of suburbia are calling loudest for is some planning, some foresight. Given the tremendous amount of building that will occur in our lifetimes, shouldn't we give some thought to where and how and why, they ask. Most suburban areas have no governmental apparatus to conduct such studies or draw up such plans. And private groups lack the authority to make them stick.

Meanwhile, by and large, suburbia continues like Topsy to "just grow."

What Do You Think?

1.   What are the advantages of cluster zoning over conventional zoning (if any)? If you were a builder, which would you use? Why?

2.   Suburbs tend to be homogeneous (very much alike, with few differences among the people who live there) in nature. Is this a good thing? If it is not, what would you do about

changing this apparent fact of suburban life? If it is a good
thing, how would you keep suburbs homogeneous?

11.   CAN THE SLUM BE MADE OVER? *

*Are there some rays of hope in the bleak picture of American slum
life? One of the bright spots involves the people of Bedford-Stuyvesant in Brooklyn. The late Senator Robert F. Kennedy was deeply
involved in a project in that area.*

One sunny morning last week nine young Negroes in blue denims
began primping and furbishing a single dilapidated house on a single
block in Brooklyn's sprawling Bedford-Stuyvesant section, one of the
nation's most crime-ridden black slums. There was something at once
stirring and depressing in the sight—as if this meager handful of unskilled
laborers aimed to rebuild, stone by stone, 640 square blocks riddled with
poverty and decay.

But, in fact, they were the visible beginning of the Bedford-Stuyvesant
Restoration Corp., the modest aegis for what is designed to be the most
sweeping and comprehensive rehabilitation effort ever brought to bear on a
single American community. With no less a guiding star than Sen. Robert
F. Kennedy, the Bedford-Stuyvesant scheme epitomizes one basic approach to slum reclamation: the concentration of powerful external
forces, both public and private, on the task of turning a living wasteland
into a booming commercial-residential complex. If the project fulfills
its vaulting ambitions, within a few years Bedford-Stuyvesant will have
been virtually reinvented. Most of its deteriorated three- and four-story
row housing will have been renovated. It will have two "superblocks" lined
to central green belts, two rehabilitation centers for skill training, a $4
million athletic and cultural center, a huge office- and shopping center
with perhaps a Macy's among the major stores. There will be some 25
new businesses, and plants, franchises for national chains, like Woolworth's,
a network of health centers, a local TV station, a four-year work-study
college. And flowing from it all, jobs, money, and expanded horizons
for the ghetto-locked inhabitants. . . .

The restoration program is indeed a breath-taking concept, thunder-
ing with high hopes—which makes some of Bedford-Stuyvesant's street-
wise citizens view it with understandable skepticism. "Another damn
agency," sneered a bearded young CORE member standing on Fulton
Street, the section's seedy main stem. "They come. They open offices . . .

---

* Excerpted from "To Save a Slum," *Newsweek,* November 20, 1967.

They go . . . I don't have no job and I ain't gonna get one. Nothin' changes."

Kennedy concedes that there is a huge barrier of doubt and apathy to break down: "Every politician has gone in there during election and made promises. You must always come to that edge with them—the promises haven't been kept."

For decades Bedford-Stuyvesant was a comfortable enclave of middle-class Brooklyn society. There are still spacious, tree-lined streets, rows of stolid brownstones and little of the blatant tawdriness of the uptown Harlem slum. But during World War II the area began a precipitous down-hill slide. Today some 400,000 people—around 90 per cent Negroes and Puerto Ricans—are packed into its 3½ square miles. Bedford-Stuyvesant suffers the city's highest infant mortality rate, highest rate of overcrowding, and almost the highest rate of crime and decrepit housing. Inevitably, it has been a seedbed of summer rioting.

Yet when Kennedy first systematically explored the section after the summer disturbances of 1966, he found some promising features to serve as a foundation for building; the stability afforded by a 15 per cent level of private home ownership, and a stubborn core of neighborhood pride. . . .

[T]he planners have scrupulously tried to restrain those prematurely aroused expectations that have proved nearly fatal to the large war on poverty. Kennedy staffer Tom Johnston explains: "Our feeling is that it would be much better to understate our goals and our hopes. It's going to be a helluva long pull."

Despite such precautions, there are already rumblings of resentment over what looks to some Negroes like one more grandiose handout by the white man. The two corporate bodies were quickly dubbed "White Board" and "Black Board." A factional fight forced reconstitution of the Black Board to broaden its community base earlier this year and there are still rankling discontents over the shakeup.

The program—still in its infancy—has wisely been walking softly and carrying large uncertainties. So far there is little visible but the first fruits of phase one—the housing-renovation project. . . .

And hope remains high, despite the certain knowledge that tangible progress may be ten years off. "I view it as a testing ground for the proposition that . . . a mixture of the private sector, government and the community can work," says one Black Board member. To that, Robert Kennedy's foremost political rival in New York adds his own amen. Says John Lindsay: "I think this is going to work."

1. Do you think that programs such as that of Bedford-Stuy-vesant can provide the solution to the slum problems of the nation? What difficulties do you see for such a plan? How would you develop neighborhood pride in a slum area? Do you think it can be done? Explain.
2. What is meant by the "private sector"? How can the private and public sectors be matched for maximum effectiveness?

12. A COMMISSION RECOMMENDS *

The Report of the National Advisory Commission on Civil Disorders had some specific recommendations to make about housing. How do you react to its ideas?

· Provision of 600,000 low and moderate-income housing units next year, and 6 million units over the next five years.

Some 6 million substandard housing units are occupied in the United States today, and well over that number of families lack sufficient income to rent or buy standard housing, without spending over 25 per cent of their income and thus sacrificing other essential needs. The problem promises to become more critical with the expanded rate of family formation on the immediate horizon and the increasing need to replace housing which has been destroyed or condemned.

In our view, the dimension of the need calls for an unprecedented national effort. We believe that the nation's housing programs must be expanded to bring within the reach of low and moderate-income families 600,000 new and existing units next year, and 6 million units over the next five years.

· An expanded and modified below-market interest rate program.

The below-market interest rate program, which makes long-term, low-interest financing available to nonprofit and limited profit sponsors, is the best mechanism presently available for engaging private enterprise in the task of providing moderate and lower-income housing. . . .

We recommend that legislation be enacted to permit interest-free loans to nonprofit sponsors to cover preconstruction costs, and to allow limited profit corporations to sell projects to nonprofit corporations, co-

* Excerpted from the *Report of the National Advisory Commission on Civil Disorders,* United States Riot Commission, March 1, 1968.

operatives, or condominiums. We also recommend that funding levels of the program be substantially increased.

· An expanded and modified rent supplement program, and an ownership supplement program.

The rent supplement program offers a highly flexible tool for subsidizing housing costs because it permits adjustment of the subsidy according to the income of the tenant. The project financing is at market rate, so that tenants who do not qualify for supplements must pay market rentals. Potentially, therefore, these developments can provide an alternative to public housing for low-income families while still attracting middle-income families.

We believe, however, that several changes are necessary if the full potential of this program is to be realized.

First, we recommend that existing regulations restricting architectural design, imposing rigid unit cost standards, and limiting tenant income to amounts lower than required by statute be removed. These regulations diminish the attractiveness of the program to private developers, and represent a major barrier to substantial expansion of the program.

Second, the statutory limitation of rent supplements to new or rehabilitated housing, should be changed to permit use of rent supplements in existing housing. In many areas, removal of the restriction would make possible a major increase of the program without requiring investment in new construction. This option must be made available if the program is to be expanded to its fullest potential.

Third, the rent supplement concept should be extended to provide home ownership opportunities for low-income families. The ambition to own one's own home is shared by virtually all Americans and we believe it is in the interest of the nation to permit all who share such a goal to realize it. Home ownership would eliminate one of the most persistent problems facing low-income families in rental housing—poor maintenance by absentee landlords—and would provide many low income families with a tangible stake in society for the first time.

· Federal write-down of interest rates on loans to private builders.

To make private loan capital available, we recommend direct federal-write-down of interest rates on market rate loans to private construction firms for moderate-rent housing. This program would make it possible for any qualified builder to enter the moderate-rent housing field on the basis of market rate financing, provided that the project meets necessary criteria.

· An expanded and more diversified public housing program.

Since its establishment in 1937, the public housing program has produced only some 650,000 low-rent housing units. Insufficient funding has prevented construction of a quantity more suited to the need, and unrealistic unit-cost limitations have mandated that most projects be of institutional design and mammoth size. The resulting large concentration of low-income families has often created conditions generating great resistance in communities to new projects of this type.

We believe that there is a need for substantially more public housing, but we believe that the emphasis of the program should be changed from the traditional publicly built, slum based, high-rise project to smaller units on scattered sites. Where traditional high-rise projects are constructed, facilities for social services should be included in the design, and a broad range of such services provided for tenants.

· An expanded Model Cities Program.

The Model Cities Program is potentially the most effective weapon in the federal arsenal for a long-term, comprehensive attack on the problems of American cities. It offers a unique means of development of local priorities, coordinating all applicable government programs—including those relating to social development (e.g., education and health) as well as physical development—and encouraging innovative plans and techniques. Its "block grant" multi-purpose funding feature allows the city to deploy program funds with much greater flexibility than is possible under typical categorical grant programs. The statutory requirement that there be widespread citizen participation and maximum employment of area residents in all phases of the program promises to involve community residents in a way we think most important.

· A reoriented and expanded urban renewal program.

Urban renewal has been an extremely controversial program since its inception. We recognize that in many cities it has demolished more housing than it has erected, and that it has often caused dislocation among disadvantaged groups.

Nevertheless, we believe that a greatly expanded but reoriented urban renewal program is necessary to the health of our cities. Urban renewal is an essential component of the Model Cities Program and, in its own right, is an essential tool for any city attempting to preserve social and economic vitality. The program has sometimes been poorly implemented, but we believe the concept is sound.

· Enactment of a national comprehensive and enforceable open-occupancy law.

The federal government should enact a comprehensive and enforceable open-occupancy law making it an offense to discriminate in the sale or rental of any housing—including single family houses on the basis of race, creed, color, or national origin.

In recent years, various piecemeal attempts have been made to deal with the problem of housing discrimination. Executive Order 11063, issued by President Kennedy in 1962, provided that agreements for federally assisted housing made after the date of the Order must be covered by enforceable nondiscrimination pledges. Congress, in enacting

Title IV of the Civil Rights Act of 1964, promulgated a broad national policy of nondiscrimination with respect to programs or activities receiving federal financial assistance—including public housing and urban renewal. Eighteen states and more than 40 cities have enacted fair housing laws of varying degrees of effectiveness.

Despite these actions, the great bulk of housing produced by the private sector remains unaffected by anti-discrimination measures. So long as this continues, public and private action at the local level will be inhibited by the argument that local action produces competitive disadvantage.

· Reorientation of federal housing programs to place more low- and moderate-income housing outside of ghetto areas.

Enactment of a national fair housing law will eliminate the most obvious barrier limiting the areas in which nonwhites live, but it will not deal with an equally impenetrable barrier, the unavailability of low and moderate-income housing in the nonghetto areas.

To date, housing programs serving low-income groups have been concentrated in the ghettos. Nonghetto areas, particularly suburbs, for the most part have steadfastly opposed low-income rent supplements, or below-market interest rate housing, and have successfully restricted use of these programs outside the ghetto.

What Do You Think?

1. The Commission calls for an "unprecedented national effort." Do you feel that such an effort is necessary? Why? Do you think that only an effort at the federal level will bring our housing up to standard? Why?

2. Many of the recommendations call for changes in the method of financing homes. Why is this such a problem? The Commission also calls for dispersing public housing throughout the city. Do you agree with this recommendation? Why?

3. Write your own set of recommendations for a housing program in the United States. Attempt to be as specific as possible.

13. THE MAYOR OF AN INDUSTRIAL CENTER CHARTS HIS COURSE *

Richard Hatcher was elected Mayor of Gary, Indiana, in 1967. His inaugural address was a call for all citizens to work together to build a new Gary.

My fellow Americans, today we are witnessing a rebirth of Gary's determination to take its rightful place among the great cities of our nation. With a resolute mind we embark upon a four-year journey, to change the face of our city and unite the hearts of our citizens; to tear down slums and build healthy bodies; to destroy crime and create beauty; to expand industry and restrict pollution.

Gary, Indiana, is a warm city—it has welcomed in large numbers into its midst emigrants from southern Europe, black people from the deep South, and those who come from south of the border. In diversity, we have found strength; however, today is a new day. Let it be known that as of this moment, there are some who are no longer welcome in Gary, Indiana. Those who have made a profession of violating our laws are no longer welcome. Those who would stick up our businessmen and rape our women are no longer welcome. Those who would bribe our policemen and other public officials and those public officials who accept bribes are no longer welcome, and those who would sow the seeds of discord and peddle the poison of racism, let it be clearly understood, are no longer welcome in Gary, Indiana.

A special word to my brothers and sisters who because of circumstances beyond your control find yourselves locked into miserable slums, without enough food to eat, inadequate clothing for your children and no hope for tomorrow. It is a primary goal of this administration to make your life better. To give you a decent place to live. To help create job opportunities for you and to assist you in every way in breaking the vicious chain of poverty. To give you your rightful share of the good life.

To our business community, including United States Steel Corporation and other large corporations, I say that Gary has been good to you, but it can be better. We assure you that this administration stands ready to support you in your efforts to rejuvenate our downtown, that it will work closely with you in attempting to attract new industry and enterprise in developing a healthy economic climate. In return, we shall ask you to roll up your sleeves and stand with us as we attempt to rebuild this city.

---

* The Hon. Richard Hatcher, Inaugural Address, Gary, Indiana, 1967.

Share with us your technical expertise, and your know-how and your money. Help us save our city. Each of you has a moral commitment to this community, and to your fellow man. And if you think so, now's the time to say so. There is nothing sacred in silence, nothing Christian in cowardice, nothing temperate in timidity.

To organized labor, we make a special plea that in the great tradition of your movement and out of your deep concern for the little man, the average man, you join us in this effort. Join us as we attempt to put into practice the great principle espoused by Samuel Gompers long ago and Joseph Germano more recently . . . "To every man his due."

To those who will be employees of this city, I say that the highest standards of integrity will be expected of you, and anyone who fails to meet that requirement will be summarily discharged. Graft and corruption shall end and efficiency shall begin.

Today we have sworn in a new city council. Represented there are men and women of integrity and great ability. I look forward to working closely with them for I am honored to call them all friend. Their responsibility is clear cut—to give you, the citizens of Gary, four years of the finest most progressive government in this city's history. To engage in constructive criticism and opposition to this administration when conscience so dictates, but never to oppose simply for opposition's sake. Our city is suffering. And unless the right medicine is administered, it may die. We have long since passed the point where either this administration or this council can afford the luxury of playing politics with the lives of our people.

To the press, we ask your understanding, patience, and help—all of our judgments shall not be correct, but they shall be honestly made. You have a responsibility not only to report the news accurately but to interpret it with restraint.

Let me for a moment speak to our young people. Your city needs you. We shall seek ways to capture your spirit, imagination, and creativity in order that they may be true assets in our city's fight to improve itself. Our future depends upon the dedication of our young people today.

And finally, to all of our citizens, whether you live in Glen Park, in midtown, or in Miller, I make a special appeal. We cannot solve our problems, we cannot save our city if we all are divided.

The great promise of our city will not be realized until we treat each other as equals without respect to race or religion. To quote our President, "Until justice is blind to color, until education is unaware of race, until opportunity is unconcerned with the color of men's skins, emancipation will be a proclamation and not a fact. The Negro today asks justice. We do not answer him when we reply by asking patience." We have talked long enough in this city about equality. The time is here to live it. If we really want good government, peace, and unity, now's the time to practice what we preach. Good government comes in assorted colors and nationalities.

Together, we shall walk through our valleys of hope; together we shall climb the steep mountains of opportunity, for we seek a high and beautiful new plateau—a new plateau of economy and efficiency in government, a new plateau of progress in government; a new plateau where every man, Democrat and Republican, rich or poor, Jew and gentile, black and white, shall live in peace and dignity.

And so my fellow Americans, as we go from this place, let us understand clearly our role and our responsibility. This is a God-given opportunity to become builders of the future instead of guardians of a barren past, and we must not waste it. Let us pray for this wisdom and guidance. Let us dare to make a new beginning. Let us shatter the walls of the ghetto for all time. Let us build a new city and a new man to inhabit it. Let each and every one of us have the courage to do what we all know must be done. For we here in Gary, Indiana, have much to say about what will happen in urban America.

Our problems are many. But our determination is great, and we feel as Tennyson must have felt when he said:

Oh yet we trust that somehow good will be the final goal of ill. . . .
That nothing walks with aimless feet
That not one life shall be destroyed
Or cast as rubbish to the void
When God hath made the pile complete.

Behold, we know not anything
I can but trust that good shall fall at last—far off—at last to all
And every winter change to spring.

And every winter change to spring. In Gary, together, we seek to change all winters to spring. We know the way is difficult, but that does not discourage us. One of America's outstanding black poets, a scholar and wise man, Professor Arna Bontemps, once wrote the following:

We are not come to make a strife
With words upon this hill;
It is not wise to waste the life
Against a stubborn will
Yet we would die as some have done,
Beating a way for the rising sun.

Gary is a rising sun. Together, we shall beat a way; together we shall turn darkness into light, despair into hope and promise into progress. For God's sake, for Gary's sake—let's get ourselves together.

What Do You Think?

    1.   Does Mayor Hatcher agree or disagree with Mayor Lindsay's statements (Reading 7 in Chapter 2)? Do you agree with his assessment of the job confronting him?

    2.   A mayor is an elected official. While the powers available to any mayor are different from those of other mayors because of the differences in local systems of government, they all have some power to deal with local problems. Do you think a mayor should have a lot of power in his city or only a little? Why? What is a mayor's most important power?

ACTIVITIES FOR INVOLVEMENT

    1.   Check the latest census of your area (either the 1960 census or a special one since that time) and attempt to develop data on your city's housing. Check the number of dilapidated houses and those without all facilities. Make a chart that indicates the figures on such conditions.

    2.   From the data you have developed and from your reading, formulate your recommendations for a sound housing policy by (a) the federal government, (b) the state government, and (c) the local government.

    3.   Organize a work team and visit the office of your city planner. Develop a time study of how he spends his day. What kinds of special problems must he deal with aside from just planning your city's future growth?

    4.   Contact the local real estate association and invite a representative to come to your classroom. Get from him his views on housing and what should be done about the housing problem of our central cities.

    5.   Some people argue that there is no racial discrimination involved in the urban housing problem. Others claim that much of the problem is caused by the refusal of whites to sell to Negroes or to lend them money with which to make home purchases. With which opinion do you agree? Conduct an investigation in your area to see if you can find evidence of discrimination.

    6.   People often base decisions upon beliefs rather than upon knowledge. Prepare a list of your beliefs about the suburbs and another list of actual facts. From your lists, attack or defend the idea "The suburban way of life is best."

4

Transportation: Can You Get There From Here?

Have you ever been on the freeway at 5:30 in the evening as people attempted to hurry home from work and shopping? Have you ever tried to find a parking place downtown in order to run in and make a small purchase? Have you ever attempted to drive from downtown to the airport and find a parking place close to the terminal?

It is an oddity of our time that the simple actions above often take longer time than a flight of 500 miles. We are able to move quickly over relatively long distances, whereas local traffic is increasingly snarled. Both situations pose a problem for our cities.

Americans love their automobiles. Somehow the family auto has become symbolic of freedom, of the ability to get somewhere, anywhere the driver wishes to go. For this reason, and because we have not as yet had time to build really modern rapid transit systems that can compete in either cost or total convenience with the auto, the freeways leading to our largest cities are clogged to overflowing morning and evening. While highway construction projects multiply, the auto industry continually increases production, to keep up with the rising demand for new cars.

We seem to be caught in a vicious cycle. The more cars there are on the road, the greater is the demand for highways and parking. As highways have grown to freeways and as entire blocks of the central city have turned into parking lots, the increased ease of driving has encouraged more and more people to use their cars. The response in some areas—Cleveland and the San Francisco Bay area, for example—has been to build rapid transit systems that hopefully will decrease auto traffic.

In some cities there has been a revolt by the citizens against the destruction of homes and living space by the freeway builders. City residents fear that their cities will become mainly highways and parking lots—even to the point where there will no longer be any reason to come to the city.

For long trips Americans are turning more and more to the air. Passengers trains are rapidly becoming a thing of the past. The great increase in air travel has created several problems for cities. Location of air terminals, control of air traffic, and access to air terminals are only three of the difficulties now being faced by city planners and transportation experts.

A future problem which will cause many headaches (literally) will be the noise of the supersonic planes as they go through the sound barrier.

Although there are many different systems of transportation, it is important that we look at transportation as one problem. The difficulties of the commuter become the difficulties of the international traveler as he attempts to go from the airport to the city. The problems of building a rapid transit system which will compete in efficiency and comfort with the private auto become the problems of millions of citizens who must pay taxes and support the system.

We shall examine some of these dilemmas next.

1. THINGS AREN'T WHAT THEY USED TO BE *

Less than 60 years ago a trip by auto across country was a real adventure. Today it is rather commonplace. Remember that in no other 60-year period in all of history have such changes occurred in man's means of transporting himself. Would a trip like the one described below be possible today?

In 1915, when I was a boy, I was invited to go along when a benevolent uncle undertook to drive from Minneapolis to Los Angeles. . . . [My] uncle took along a truck full of tents, cots, and so on. We camped along the way, all the way, partly because it was fun but mostly because in all the world there was not a motel, a tourist cabin, or a trailer park. The empty yards that surrounded country schoolhouses made good camping sites, as I recall it: there was plenty of room, and there were sanitary facilities of a sort. In the emptier reaches of Wyoming

---

* Excerpted from the introduction to "Ocean to Ocean—by Automobile," by Bruce Catton, *American Heritage,* April, 1962. © Copyright 1962 by American Heritage Publishing Co., Inc. Reprinted by permission.

and Nevada the party simply pulled off the road and camped in the sagebrush.

Finding the way was sometimes a problem, because there were no road maps and no route numbers. Our party had three cars—two touring cars and that truck—and the lead car carried packets of confetti; when it made a turn at a fork in the road, it tossed out a few handfuls so that the following cars would know which turn to take. The cars usually stayed half a mile apart, because between Minneapolis and San Francisco, there was not one mile of paved road outside of the cities and the dust a car could leave behind it was something to experience. All of the women in the parties wore long linen dusters, and the men wore khaki. Most of us wore goggles as a matter of routine.

I mentioned "touring cars." They were open cars with collapsible tops, carrying side curtains which could be buttoned in place if it rained. The closed car with glass windows was strictly for city driving then; those bumpy roads would have shattered the glass in short order on a cross-country trip. It may be in place to mention that my uncle had a chauffeur, who was very busy every single evening adjusting the motors, repairing tires, and doing other things that made it possible for us to keep moving. Flat tires, of course, were literally everyday affairs.

Nobody hurried on a cross-country trip. We averaged about one hundred miles a day, which was considered a bit leisurely but not very much so. It might be remembered that most of the roads between Iowa and California were all but totally unimproved. You couldn't make time on such roads if you wanted to, and if you tried you quickly broke something—a spring, a hip, or something.

Obviously this was not much like motoring today. It was a great deal less comfortable, but somehow it was more fun. And some of us who are now doddering peacefully down the sunset slope look back on those days with a queer fondness. You can do absolutely anything with a car nowadays—except do what we did back before the First World War.

What Do You Think?

1. The trip described was not like motoring today "but somehow it was more fun." What do you think the author had in mind when he made this statement? Would you agree with him? Explain.

2. Could you make a similar kind of journey today?

2. THE END OF A LOVE AFFAIR *

Many observers of the American scene have claimed that the average
American is caught up in a great love affair with his automobile.
This author, however, says that the affair is over. Would you agree?

Once upon a time, the American met the automobile and fell in
love. Unfortunately, this led him into matrimony, and so he did not
live happily ever after. Cooler heads could have told him the affair
was doomed from the start, for in the beginning, the American was
poorly prepared to make judgments in such matters. He was merely
a rustic Merry Andrew with a cowlick and an adolescent tightening in
the groin. In his libidinous innocence, he saw the automobile only as
curious, exciting—and obviously willing. Wherefore, he joyfully leaped
upon her, and she responded to his caresses by bolting about the landscape in what can only be called a succession of bumps and grinds.

This Arcadian idyll did not persist, of course. Had he loved her
and left her, all would have been well. Had he restrained himself, and
viewed her as a possible hired woman to be trained for work about the
farm and otherwise left strictly alone, all would have been better. But
he was innocent; she handed him a likely story and led him to the
preacher. Then, before they were fairly out of the churchyard, she
began to demonstrate less enchanting aspects of her character. The American, it seems, was trapped by a schemer.

Quickly, the automobile became the nagging wife, demanding rub-
bings and shinings and gifts. She put eyebrows over her windshield in
the 1920s, plucked them out in the late 1930s, put them on again in
the middle 1940s, and took them off once more in the 1950s. She nagged
him for bits of chrome and cursed him for his extravagance when he
brought them home. She lifted her face—expensively—from year to year;
incessantly demanded new gauds and different colors, developed ever
more costly eating habits, threatened to break the family budget and often
succeeded, and the American—poor dolt, not only catered to her whims
but decked her out in door-edge guards and silvery Kleenex dispensers.

Since woman from the dawn of time has regarded man as she
regards an old house—that is, as something to make over—it is not
surprising to note that the automobile wrought dramatic changes in her
spouse. Nevertheless, the speed and thoroughness of the transformation
is a little awe-inspiring, bespeaking either a weakness on the American's

---

* Excerpted from John Keats, *The Insolent Chariots*. Copyright © 1958 by
John Keats. Reprinted by permission of J. B. Lippincott Company.

part or a fantastic singleness of purpose on the part of the automobile, or both. For example, in fifty-eight short years the automobile not only became our nation's greatest single topic of conversation, but also unquestionably central to our economy. The automobile became demonstrably more important to us than our human wives, children, jobs, and even our food. . . . The automobile changed our dress, manners, social customs, vacation habits, the shape of our cities, consumer purchasing patterns, [and] common tastes. . . .

As the frightful marriage wore on, the automobile's original appeal shrank in inverse proportion to the growth of her demands. She grew sow-fat while demanding bigger, wider, smoother roads. The bigger and better the road, the fatter she became, and the fatter she grew, the greater her demands for even bigger roads. Then, with all the subtlety of a madam affecting a lorgnette, she put tail fins on her overblown bustle and sprouted wavering antennae from each fin. And, of course, her every whim was more costly than the last.

In view of these metamorphoses, it is understandable that the American began to stray. In the mid-1950s, he eyed the European car, and found her good. She was petite, she was new, she was gay, she was inexpensive, she bumped and she ground, and like all mistresses, she promised prestige. Maintaining a mistress when one is married to a Harpy is, however, an intolerable situation, and so we can say that the American's marriage to the American automobile is now at an end, and it is only a matter of minutes to the final pistol shot, although who pulls the trigger has yet to be determined.

What Do You Think?

1. A writer once said that Americans buy cars for their sexual symbolism. A convertible is the symbol of a mistress to the man who wishes to be a free bachelor type; a sedan is the symbol of wife and family to the conservative home-loving man, etc. Do you agree with this idea? Who decides what kind of car your family will buy?

2. Make a list of the problems caused by the growth in the number of automobiles in this country. Make a list of the advantages brought to the country by the auto. Which list outweighs the other? Should we restrict automobile production? Why or why not?

3. SOME TAXPAYERS SAY "NO!" *

Some cities have resisted the highway planners' attempts to create new freeways. The most famous revolt has taken place in San Francisco, where there is even talk of tearing down one section of elevated freeway because it destroys the view of a famous landmark.

"The time will come," Aldous Huxley has predicted in *Brave New World,* "when man will reckon the time 'in the year of our Ford.' "

That date may not be so far off in southern California, as reports projecting a 57 per cent upsurge in traffic for Los Angeles by 1985 suggest.

But here in scenic San Francisco—hotbed of the first "freeway revolt"—officials intend to buck the trend. They're banking on a new rapid-transit system to show the way.

Citizens in this port city first rose up to battle the Embarcadero Freeway in 1959. They dubbed the double-decked, wharfwide super-highway "the Concrete Monster."

At first, California highway officials conceived of the freeway as a one-deck, six lane, elevated route along the Embarcadero—with an underpass beneath the Ferry Building plaza. The design resembled Manhattan's West Side Highway.

Then a report on the city's 1980 "traffic demand" convinced engineers to doubledeck the highway, thus creating eight traffic lanes.

Neither California nor the Federal Bureau of Public Roads would agree to finance the extra $11 million needed to tunnel underneath the plaza. The board of supervisors also refused to pay the higher price of good design.

DOUBLE DECK APPROVED

So officials approved the double deck in front of the Ferry Building though even many highway engineers consider it garish.

San Franciscans were appalled. Soon their mood changed to open revolt against freeways, as former Mayor John F. Shelley informed Congress last November.

"The people are saying, 'Cut it out; no more' " he told the Senate subcommittee on roads. "The people are also questioning whether highways alone can or should do the job of moving people."

"Proposed new freeways," he added, "are regarded by many as rivers of noise, exhaust, gas, and constant never-ceasing motion: a 'river to be kept away from my door.' "

When the Mayor and his aides discussed a new freeway through residential areas, parks, and other scenic vistas, citizens signed petitions and stormed city hall in opposition.

As a result, City Hall joined the protest. The board of supervisors turned back at least $250 million in federal highway aid in 1966. The move left the Embarcadero Freeway half built, its last exit ramp releasing traffic into the downtown business district.

BOND ISSUE APPROVED

Four years earlier, voters approved a $792 million bond issue to finance the 75 mile Bay Area Rapid Transit District system now under construction. The new highspeed trains will also serve Alameda and Contra Costa counties across the San Francisco Bay area.

'FREEWAYS DON'T MOVE PEOPLE'

"The freeways move cars," [Mayor Alioto] said, "but they don't move people."

The Mayor recalled traffic surveys taken on the busy Bay Bridge to Oakland. They showed that although 130,000 vehicles cross the bridge daily, the average car carried only 1.4 people during rush hours.

But transbay buses—which make up a mere 3 per cent of the bridge traffic flow—carry 45 per cent of the rush-hour load. The BART system trains are expected to lift this figure even higher.

These statistics helped convince Mayor Alioto to oppose a plan to doubledeck the Golden Gate Bridge. He holds that the project would only create greater pressure for more freeways.

"We just don't think we owe that much to the automobile," he says.

*   *   *   *   *

Mayor Alioto also dreams of launching a high-speed ferry boat service in San Francisco Bay to serve commuters. The hydrofoil boats would travel at speeds up to 26 knots in an open attempt to lure motorists off the freeways.

The Golden Gate Bridge and Highway District warns, though, that ferry boats would run up "a fantastic deficit" and need a vast parking lot and transfer points at the terminals.

MOTORIST THE KEY

The district, chief booster of the plan to doubledeck the Golden Gate Bridge, ruled out the notion of extending the BART system to Marin County via the bridge. It strongly favors exclusive lanes for express buses, if and when the second deck is built.

"It has long been known," the district's spokesman cautioned last year, "that for the success of any mass transit system, the California motorist has to be enticed—and not forced—from his car to mass transit."

In his campaign for the Mayor's seat, however, Mr. Alioto spoke forcibly on this issue.

"The unlimited use of automobiles within the city should not be permitted or encouraged," he declared, echoing the view of New York's Mayor John V. Lindsay.

"San Francisco's various 'freeway revolts' clearly show that the people of this city do not want their neighborhoods dug up or divided by freeways."

The reform-minded Mayor insists that he is not "anti-automobile." Yet he told voters last fall:

LOBBYISTS GRUMBLING

"Autos these days are named for sleek animals, most of them dangerous. But they shouldn't panic a city like San Francisco into building more monsters like the Embarcadero Freeway."

California highway lobbyists are grumbling about plans afoot to tax commuters and parking-lot owners to firm up BART's fiscal structure. There is another side to that issue. The San Francisco Department of City Planning pointed to it in 1967.

"Each additional automobile entering the downtown during the rush hour," it maintained "requires an additional investment in street and parking space amounting to $25,000. The carrying charges on this investment work out to about four dollars per round trip per automobile."

BART planners use these figures to claim that each year their train system will save San Francisco $3.6 million by diverting transbay autos from the downtown streets.

The savings will exceed $7 million, these officials say, if diverted local traffic is taken into account.

MAJOR SWITCH FORECAST

BART's computer estimates show one of every three Bay Area commuters forsaking his car, once the 70-m.p.h. train network is complete. A full 30 per cent of the train's passengers are expected to be former bay bridge auto patrons.

If these projections prove correct, they will reflect the strongest crossover to rapid transit yet observed in the Americas. By way of comparison:

Toronto's Yonge Street subway draws 12.9 per cent of its patronage from former auto users.

Chicago's new Congress Street Rapid and Skokie Swift lines have broken 12.5 per cent and 17.5 per cent of their passengers of the driving habit, respectively.

BART hopes to more than double the drawing power of the Toronto and Chicago subways by diverting roughly 21,000 transbay auto riders to trains a day in 1975.

FORECAST DEFENDED

"This expectation is not unwarranted," BART planners said confidently last October, "in the light of high operating speeds and the forth-right appeal to motorists in passenger comfort and amenities being built into the BART facility."

If BART's predictions come true, its trains will lure 3,200 "peak hour" vehicles off the bay bridge each day in 1975—more than two lanes of bridge traffic.

Even greater relief will appear with removal of 80 per cent of San Francisco's transbay buses and 90 per cent of those based in Alameda County.

ANOTHER WHOLE BRIDGE

"The overall effect of BART, therefore," its planners promise, "will be the equivalent of seven transbay lanes in the peak hour/peak direction.

"In other words, BART will be equal to another bay bridge in delivering East Bay residents to downtown San Francisco every morning."

What Do You Think?

1. Many cities are talking about rapid transit systems that would link an entire metropolitan area. What arguments can you think of against such a system?

2. One of the important questions in the various freeway disputes is the right of freeway planners to tell citizens what is best for them. The planners are employees of the people, but they are also experts at their jobs. They want their recommendations to be accepted, whereas the people wish to maintain a final say in such matters. What arguments can you develop on both sides of this issue?

4.   THE DRIVE TO BREAK TRAFFIC JAMS *

As traffic problems multiply, so do ideas for dealing with them. Now the federal government is spearheading a drastic attack on the traffic crush. Which of the ideas below seem most practicable?

Rush-hour traffic in more and more U. S. cities is getting so snarled that the Government in Washington has decided to take a direct hand in untangling the mess.

Latest tack: speeding up the flow of cars, buses and trucks on existing streets to relieve congestion far more quickly than this can be done by building new roads. . . .

WHAT THE U. S. IS DOING NOW

Just getting under way, for smaller cities, is a federal program to finance broader use of simple, but effective measures to unclog traffic. Among the proposals:

· Flexible signals that stay green longer on main arteries during heavy traffic or that are timed to permit drivers to move steadily at a set speed.

· Reversible middle lanes with overhead signals that direct autos one way during the morning rush hour, and the opposite way in the evening crush.

· Lanes set aside for exclusive use by busses—curb lanes on city streets, inside ones on urban freeways.

· Construction of extra lanes at downtown intersections for cars making left or right turns, thus removing bottlenecks for other autos.

"Mass transit and urban expressways may be the long-term answers to the national traffic jam," says a high executive of the U. S. Department of Transportation, "but commuters don't want to wait till 1970 or 1980 for a fast, comfortable ride to work."

A LOOK AHEAD

New efforts to untangle downtown congestion take on added urgency in light of the latest official forecasts.

By 1975, . . . there will be 26 million more motor vehicles in the U. S. than there are today. That will be an increase of more than one-fourth.

---

* Excerpted from "The Drive in U. S. to Break Traffic Jams," *U. S. News & World Report,* October 23, 1967. © 1967 U. S. News & World Report Corporation.

Half of all traffic moves on city streets that make up just 13 per cent of all highway mileage in the country. And the prospect is for the volume of traffic on these streets to increase faster than on the rest of the roadways. . . .

BAN ON STREET PARKING?

Maneuvering into and out of curb parking spaces, authorities say, impedes the flow of traffic, too.

More and more cities are banning parking on main streets, at least during rush hours.

ELECTRONIC CONTROL

On streets and highways themselves, officials bank on growing use of electronic devices to increase the volume and speed of traffic that can be handled.

For an idea of what is in store for major cities, look at Chicago's Eisenhower Expressway, which has a project financed in part with federal funds.

Electronic detectors along a 5-mile stretch of the freeway measure traffic and feed the information to a central computer. The computer then operates signal lights on entrance ramps to regulate the flow of vehicles entering the freeway, feeding cars into gaps in traffic that occur even during rush hours.

The traffic signals tell the driver when to stop, when to go and what speed to reach as he moves into the gap.

The result, say officials, is a steady movement of autos that has cut the period of evening-hour congestion from 2½ to 1½ hours, while increasing traffic volume by 25 per cent.

Albert B. Kelley, a spokesman for the Federal Highway Administration, says:

"It was like adding a fourth lane to the present three lanes of expressway. The investment was $800,000, compared with about 10 million dollars per mile for much urban freeway construction."

A similar system is being tested on a 6½-mile stretch of the Gulf Freeway leading into Houston. There 14 closed-circuit TV cameras monitor traffic and regulate the flow of cars into inbound lanes during the morning rush hour. The cameras also help city police spot accidents and car breakdowns that threaten the traffic flow.

Besides speeding up the movement of autos by more than 50 per cent, the system has reduced crashes on the controlled stretch of highway by 35 to 45 per cent, according to William R. McCasland, the project director.

On Detroit's John C. Lodge Freeway, TV surveillance is used to determine what speed to flash on overhead signals to insure the steadiest flow for a given volume of automobiles.

More-advanced plans are in the works. The head of research for the Bureau of Public Roads, has this to say:

"Today's systems can speed traffic along a given road. Now we want to route the driver to alternate roads that are less crowded."

Devices are being developed for a "second-generation" ramp-control system, for possible testing in Los Angeles. Before getting into line on an entrance ramp, the motorist may see a sign that shunts him to a less-traveled parallel street or expressway.

The next step, according to Mr. Baker: a device, built right into an automobile, which receives signals telling the driver the fastest way to get to a specified destination.

Such a setup has already been tested. General Motors and Philco-Ford have Government contracts to develop an actual system to be used on a roadway network in a large American city.

Highway officials say traffic can be speeded up with much less elaborate devices, by broader application of engineering, techniques already in use in many big metropolitan areas.

Under a pilot program begun this year, the Government is footing half the bill for a dozen cities—from Augusta, Me., to Lincoln, Nebr.— that adopt proven measures of traffic control. Other cities will be added later.

Federal aid, under the program, will be available for such things as:

· Building bridges and tunnels at major intersections to separate pedestrian from motor traffic.

· Carving indented bays out of sidewalks or roadsides for busses and trucks to load and unload, thus allowing other vehicles to move straight through. Shelters could be built to protect waiting bus passengers in bad weather.

· Traffic signals and signs that are needed to establish one-way streets or no-parking zones, as well as for reversible middle lanes and for extra turning lanes at intersections.

All these innovations and others still to come are counted on by planners to help solve a traffic problem that grows worse day by day.

What Do You Think?

1. There seems to be a long-range solution to the traffic problems accepted by many experts. What is it? Do you think it will work in your area? Why or why not?

2.   Some of the plans for the short-term solution of the problem involve use of modern technology. As they are described, which do you think offers the most promise? Why?

5.   A TRAFFIC JAM—IN THE AIR! *

While there are problems in our ability to go short distances, we also have transportation difficulties with longer trips. Does this sound familiar?

A Monday morning in October, unseasonably warm, visibility excellent. No apparent reason why the gleaming jet at Newark Airport cannot take off on schedule for Washington.

A passenger seated in the handsome new DC-9-30, one of a fleet which Eastern Air Lines has just bought for its intercity shuttle service, picks some literature out of the seat pocket in front of him.

He reads that the DC-9-30 is capable of flying 520 m.p.h. His schedule, however, says that takeoff time is 8:30, and landing time is 9:20. Why so long to fly 250 miles? The passenger, through long experience, knows that the airline must allow extra time for taxiing, clearing the field, takeoff, and possible delays.

Even so, Eastern has been optimistic. Monday mornings are exceptionally busy. Air traffic backs up on the ground and overhead. The captain's voice crackles over the intercom. He apologizes, says there will be "a few minutes delay." Minutes tick on. An hour goes past before the craft roars down the runway for takeoff.

With its 520 m.p.h. capacity, the jet can make up some of the lost time. But not an hour's worth.

PROBLEM CALLED CRISIS

The passenger fidgets, grumbles, then settles back resignedly. He has an 11 o'clock appointment in Washington, but based on past experience, he has allowed for such a delay. Soon the plane banks into a turn over National Airport.

The captain's voice again. More apologies. Traffic has backed up. The jet must go into the stack for another "few minutes." The passenger squirms, glances anxiously at his watch. Twenty minutes later the plane settled into its landing glide.

It is 10:30 when the passenger bolts from the plane, through the terminal, and grabs a cab. He is just in time for his appointment.

This incident, repeated countless times over, is the red flag that

---

* From George H. Favre, "Air Travelers Hurry to Wait." Reprinted by permission from *The Christian Science Monitor.* © 1968 The Christian Science Publishing Society. All rights reserved.

should warn the flying public of impending trouble. Like the top of an iceberg, airline delays are only the visible top 10 per cent of a mountain of problems. Lumped together they add up to what [former] Secretary of Transportation Alan S. Boyd terms a national airport crisis: Among these troubles:

· Increasing congestion in the air over and around major commercial airports and with this congestion, increasing difficulty in maintaining minimum safety margins.

· Increasing congestion on the ground. This includes congestion of planes on runways, taxiing strips, and aprons. It also involves overtaxed parking, terminal, ticketing, baggage, and other passenger facilities.

· The chronic and worsening problem of moving passengers between airports and city centers.

· Increasing levels of aircraft noise over residential areas around airports.

· A growing load on the already overtaxed personnel who man air-control facilities at airport towers and regional centers.

· Mounting opposition to the freedom of general aviation—a catch-all category that covers everything from a Piper Cub to a 10-passenger corporation-owned jet—to use the facilities of major commercial air-ports.

· The constant preoccupation of airlines, airport operators and governments at all levels with the problem of getting money to pay for urgently needed new facilities.

The inconvenience suffered by passengers in delayed takeoffs and landings is the price they pay for the other problems. Air passengers literally mark time while all the contributory problems are resolved. In 1965 they marked time for 20 million minutes.

One reason—some would say excuse—for this endless waiting line is to ensure safety. The Federal Aviation Agency (FAA) concedes that its rules for dealing with congestion may result in increasing delays, but insists that they preserve at least minimum standards of safety.

That is the official FAA position. But some groups, such as the Air Line Pilot Association (ALPA) insist that safety standards are in fact being steadily lowered by the FAA. Says Thomas A. Basnight, Jr., director of regulatory matters for the ALPA: "The FAA is leading us down a trail of lowering operating weather minimums to zero-zero. Right now we have minimums low enough to lead aircraft into weather conditions serious enough to interfere with surface vehicles' operation."

Weather, of course, is a prime delay factor in aviation.

NEAR MISSES RISE

Mr. Basnight also insists that increasing congestion in the air-space over major airports is itself an unsafe condition, causing a growing number of "near misses." He says of these: "I believe near misses are increasing at about the same pace as new aircraft enter operations."

It was charged last fall that the FAA had reported 82 near midair collisions in the New York metropolitan area over 2½ years, 36 of them involving a general aviation aircraft. Since the reporting system is voluntary, and many pilots do not report "near misses" for fear of punitive action, said Mr. Rosenthal, the total of reported misses falls far short of actual occurrences.

TIME SAME AS PROP PLANES

For all these reasons, air travelers cannot take delays lightly or philosophically. Delay on the ground or in the air is a sign that all is not well in the national air system. . . .

Yet delays are of themselves a serious problem. For passengers, an increase in the occurrence of delay means that they must make ever larger allowances for travel time.

Delays are costly to airlines, too. Observes an Eastern Air Lines executive: "We have to allow the same time on our new scheduled jet flights today as we allowed on the old prop jobs 10 years ago."

That's a poor return for a heavy investment in the expensive high-speed jets. Eastern has just bought 14 of the DC-9-30's at $3.7 million each for its shuttle service.

DELAYS COSTLY

For the airline, each extra minute on the ground or in the air costs many dollars. The bigger the plane, the more the delays cost. The FAA has estimated that delays in peak traffic hours at John F. Kennedy International Airport in New York cost airlines more than $1,500 an hour.

The 20 million minutes of delay experienced by the United States air fleet in 1965 cost airlines an estimated $64 million in fuel, pilot time, and other costs. And since then air traffic has jumped more than 25 per cent.

Despite the high cost of delays to airlines, they have the ability to resolve the problem at least partially at their own discretion. That answer is to reschedule flights.

But competitive reasons keep them from taking steps to reschedule flights in such a way as to even out the traffic flow over the day and reduce congestion at peak hours.

RESCHEDULE ACCENTED

The Secretary of Transportation told the Senate Commerce Subcommittee on Aviation that the possibility of such rescheduling has not been given enough attention.

Airlines object to any attempt to reschedule flights away from peak hours. They figure businessmen want to fly out early in the morning on a breakfast flight and arrive in early evening in time to have supper at home with the family.

Secretary Boyd told Congress: "I believe . . . now that the average air passenger will be quite ready to consider a flight at an odd hour if he can avoid the aggravation of trying to move during the conventional hours." He urged incentives for off-hours flights such as cheaper fares.

Such incentives are already in wide use, especially in family plans. Here lower fares are offered for family groups except on weekends. Eastern Air Lines offers a $3 saving on off-hour flights in its Boston-New York-Washington shuttle service.

AIRPORT INCENTIVES URGED

Beyond airlines offering incentives to travelers to fly off hours, Mr. Boyd suggests that airport operators do the same for the airlines. This could be done either by raising airport landing charges and other service fees provided during peak hours, . . . or by limiting use of the airport at peak hours to the most productive users—that is, the commercial aircraft carrying heavy passenger loads.

If some of these ideas require changes in the laws or regulations he added, "we must be prepared to move ahead with such changes."

One thing is certain. Whether through rescheduling or some other means, airport congestion must be relieved before saturation is total. No one wants to have this point brought home by more air disasters.

What Do You Think?

1. While there is a problem today with overcrowded airports, it will become even worse in the future. What would you suggest as a solution?

2. Jet airliners of the future are going to require longer runways than those of today. This creates a problem of land use. Some people argue that there is really no need for superjets and that too much land is already used by airports. Others say that the land must be found and that air travel must expand. What do you say? Explain.

6.   SOME SUGGESTED SOLUTIONS *

Technological developments suggest ways of easing our air transport problems. Here are some of those developments.

Somewhere in the wilds of Malaya, a squat plane flits across the tree-tops and suddenly dips to a quick, short landing in what appears to be a mere patch of grass amidst the trees.

An observer unacquainted with short takeoff and landing (STOL) planes like the five passenger Helio Courier, might think that the little single-engined craft had crashed into the trees at the other end of the clearing, for lack of runway.

But STOL planes have been making such tight-squeeze landings for years. They have served bush pilots, missionaries, and combat troops in jungle wars. They now are being used in Vietnam.

Along with the VTOLs (vertical takeoff and landing craft) more familiarly known as helicopters, STOLs are one of the more promising solutions to the problem of air congestion in the United States.

Right now, of course, helicopters are being used in major cities around the country to transport air travelers—those prepared to pay the price—from city centers to nearby airports.

BUSY CORRIDOR

But the new frontier in commercial aviation is the short haul from city center to city center—bypassing the major airports completely and using landing pads (for VTOLs) or short runways from 300 to 1,500 feet (for STOLs).

Take the Northeast corridor, for example. Within a 500 mile coastal strip are such major cities as Boston, New York, Philadelphia, Baltimore, and Washington. Together they have the heaviest air traffic of any corridor in the nation. In fact, one-third of all the domestic air traffic going out of New York goes to one of the other four cities.

If a workable short haul, low flying air system could be built in under the high flying system serving major cities, it would cut back air congestion tremendously. Such a cutback would add years of potential expansion to the rapidly clogging Northeast corridor's major airports.

If all goes well, this could come about, say experts, within a decade. Ideally, it would have been developed by now. But progress has been

---

halting. Research and progress development on V/STOL planes . . . large enough to do the job has not yet broken through technical difficulties. A workable system needs planes capable of carrying from 50 to 120 passengers.

One promising design is the 56 passenger French Breguet 941, a four engined STOL craft that cruises at 285 mph. It is still in the testing stage. Some American STOL models are also in the works.

Most experts favor STOLs over VTOLs for an intercity system. Their obvious drawback is that they require more landing room.

AVAILABLE SPACE

STOLs, with their need for 300 to 1,500 feet of runway, have their own obvious drawbacks in the downtown area of cities where land costs may run $40 or $60 or more a square foot. But that problem is not insoluble.

Both the scheduled airlines and the cities which may be served by a shorthaul intercity system are already thinking in terms of where to put "STOLports" and how to regulate their use.

Depending on the city and its particular needs and potentials there is a wide range of possible STOLport sites. In a land scarce, heavily congested area like New York, with waterfront space, an obvious answer is to use man-made islands or docks in the water. Airspace over railroad yards is another possibility. Rooftops, like the Pan Am Building, offer a solution where the noise problem does not raise insurmountable problems for City Hall.

Farther out at the edge of the city, shopping plaza, industrial parks, and highways are further possible STOLport sites.

Samuel J. Solomon, a patriarchal innovator of the aviation field, has just patented plans for a combination office, transportation center, parking and hotel complex whose common roof would form a V/STOL-port. Mr. Solomon visualizes it in a decaying section of Washington or New York. It would sound like pie in the sky, except for the fact that Mr. Solomon has been doing this kind of thing throughout his aviation career.

Founder and president of several airlines at various times, including Northeast, the originator of helicopter passenger and mail feeder service, and former manager of Washington National Airport, he has a proven practical head for air service innovation.

A study by the Center for Transportation Studies at Eagleton Institute, part of Rutgers University in New Brunswick, N. J., came up with the "aquadromes" as an answer to the STOLport situation in New York. These would be saucer-shaped floating islands, anchored in the river, and would cost from $5 to $10 million each.

Whatever shape such STOLports may eventually take, and whoever may build and operate them, the commercial airlines are moving ahead on the premise that short haul intercity air service is their next frontier of major expansion. . . .

Some crucial questions remain. One of the hardest is what safety standards must be set for new-design planes. One example is the compound helicopter—reminiscent of the Autogiro—which combines wings and forward propulsion engines with the familiar "chopper" blades that give vertical flight. When such craft make the transition from fast forward flight to slow speed approach and hover flight, what performance characteristics are acceptable? No one knows for sure, as yet, nor will they until actual prototypes are flown and tested.

What Do You Think?

1.   How does the development of STOLs and VTOLs help solve the problems raised in Reading 5 ? Do you think the low-flying system will work?

2.   It is possible that new types of planes will bring about more growth in the suburbs and extend the suburbs to greater distances from the central city. Would this development solve the air transport problem of cities in the United States? Explain.

7.   A GOAL TO WORK TOWARD *

In planning transportation systems, there are some ideas which have to be kept in mind. Consider the following:

We need to know more than we do about the desirable size and character of labor markets, and about business linkages. For most economic purposes, however, it seems reasonably evident that a large metropolitan area can be broken down into smaller functional units.

Two principles for transportation policy are proposed:

(1) The first is a motto: remember that mobility is not usually an end in itself, but a means to other ends. Vacation travel may sometimes be a positive pleasure, but an extra ten miles on the journey to work is a costly nuisance.

(2) The second follows from the motto: transportation planning

---

* Excerpted from Catherine Bauer Wurster, "Framework for an Urban Society," *Goals for Americans* © 1960 by the American Assembly, Columbia University, New York, N. Y. Reprinted by permission of Prentice-Hall, Inc., Englewood Cliffs, N. J.

must be carefully coordinated with other kinds of planning, to shape a desirable development pattern. Such a pattern is likely to be one that maximizes convenience rather than mobility.

What Do You Think?

Are these principles valid? Should they be taken into account in planning? What additional thoughts to guide planners would you suggest?

ACTIVITIES FOR INVOLVEMENT

1.   Invite a member of an automobile dealers association to come to class to talk about the views of the dealers and producers relative to freeways and the expansion of automobile use.

2.   Arrange a field trip to the air control center at the local airport. At the same time, talk with some pilots and an airline company representative. Check the viewpoints of these people for agreements and disagreements.

3.   Arrange a debate on the following question: Resolved: Federal funds for highways should be cut by one-half and spent on rapid transit systems serving the major metropolitan areas.

4.   Form a transportation committee to develop a proposal that will allow passengers to get from downtown to the airport in 40 minutes. Have the committee illustrate its proposal with appropriate maps, charts, and sketches.

5.   Conduct a survey among a random sample of students as to whether or not they would ride a rapid transit system, and why. Tally the results as well as the reasons they offer pro and con. Now conduct a second survey among a random sample of adults in the community at large. Again tally the responses and reasons given. How do the two lists compare? Hold a class discussion on how to explain any differences and similarities noted.

6.   Listed below are a number of actions that could be taken to deal with the problem of air congestion.
   · The number of people flying could be limited to those who have important business.
   · Certain days of the week could be closed to all air traffic except major airlines.
   · People living near airports could be moved.
   · Very strict regulations on air traffic could be adopted.
   · Certain hours of every day could be prohibited to *any* air traffic.
   · Larger aircraft could be developed.
   · Airlines could be restricted as to the *number* of flights they could offer per day.

· People could be paid *not* to fly, but to travel by some other means of transportation.

· The federal government could offer subsidies to railroads to improve their service.

Rank these suggestions as to their feasibility. Then write a brief paper (two pages maximum) as to which you think offers the most and which the least promise—and why.

5

Pollution: Our Poisoned Environment

Life seemingly holds more excitement for more people than ever before in history. Yet the very air we breathe presents a major problem to man. And the waters we depend upon for drinking, for agriculture, and for recreation are clouded with pollutants which can cause incalculable harm.

Air and water pollution are but two aspects of the tremendous challenge imposed by our mass production and mass consumption way of life. Another is the disposal of waste—garbage, old cars, and other discards from our prolific technology. By virtue of sheer productivity, we are faced with a crisis in our environment.

Like many of the problems of modern man, air pollution is not particularly new. King Edward I of England set forth a law limiting the burning of coal in 1273. Since that time, there have been numerous attempts to clean up the air. London, Germany, Chicago, and California are just some of the places where law-making bodies have attempted to control the quality of air breathed by their citizens.

Air can become polluted by foreign matter from camp fires, burning trash, industrial waste, automobile exhaust fumes, or atomic waste matter. Each improvement in technology seems to create new problems of waste disposal. Currently, the increase in the numbers of automobiles is causing great concern.[f] Along with this growth has come an alarming increase in the incidence of lung cancer.

The evidence is indisputable: polluted air can cause illness and death. The damage can be done quickly or over a long period of time. In 1948 in Donora, Pennsylvania, 18 people died and thousands more were made ill by waste matter that persisted in the air for several days. In London, England, in 1952, smoke, soot, and fog hung over the city for a week. In that time over 4,000 deaths were attributed to the aerial wastes, and many more lives were shortened by resultant illnesses.

Our federal government is aware of the problem. A staff report to a United States Senate committee states: "There is strong evidence that air pollution is associated with a number of respiratory ailments. These include (1) nonspecific infectious upper respiratory disease, (2) chronic bronchitis, (3) chronic constrictive ventilatory disease, (4) pulmonary emphysema, (5) bronchial asthma, and (6) lung cancer." On the state and local level, authorities are also concerned about the menace. Strong programs have been adopted in Pittsburgh, Pennsylvania; St. Louis, Missouri; and Los Angeles, California. The state government in California has established controls on automobile exhausts which are stronger than federal controls passed in 1967.

Paying for control can be done through tax-supported efforts, as in Los Angeles and San Francisco, or it can be done by forcing the owner-offender to provide for safe elimination of wastes. Either way the individual citizen will ultimately pay the bill, for the factory or utility owner will pass on his increased costs in the form of higher prices. In the final analysis, it is the average citizen who must decide for himself how much clean air is worth.

In some areas water pollution is a critical problem. The Ohio River Valley Sanitation Commission, formed by eight states in 1948, has had some success in cleaning up this once beautiful river. Before the formation of the commission, over 1,000 cities had been dumping raw sewage into the Ohio. There are still problems to be overcome before the river is returned to its former condition.

Lake Erie illustrates a similar problem, as does the Lake Tahoe area within California and between California and Nevada. Water pollution is linked to the inadequate systems of sewers in our cities, but this is only a part of the problem. Industrial waste accounts for at least as much of our water pollution. Water is used in prodigious quantities in many industrial processes and is then returned, loaded with wastes, to streams, rivers, or lakes.

Even new farming techniques provide a source of water pollution. Since the invention of DDT in the early 1940's, many new chemical compounds have been discovered which control harmful insects but which in turn may be harmful to man or wildlife. The use of chemical fertilizers appears to result in an increase in the algae found in waters receiving such chemicals, a process still little understood.

Atomic waste materials may be an important future source of pollution. At present such waste is buried or dumped sealed in concrete containers in the oceans. As the United States increases its use of atomic power, the amount of such waste will greatly increase. New methods of disposal will have to be found.

The problems imposed by pollution of the environment are very difficult. Often people prefer not to act until the situation becomes an obvious threat. This can be too late. Our increasing population and our increasingly technological society are going to create more and more waste matter. Somehow, this waste must be disposed of if it is not to prove a serious menace to man and to the good life he wishes to lead.

1. POLLUTION IS NO NEW PROBLEM *

Pollution and concern for the quality of life have been written and talked about for many years. Here is poet James Thomson's view of the city. How would you describe this view?

What men are they who haunt these fatal glooms
    And fill their living mouths with dust to death,
And make their habitations in the tombs,
    And breathe eternal sighs with mortal breath,
And pierce life's pleasant veil of various error
To reach that void of darkness and old terror
    Wherein expire the lamps of hope and faith?
Unspoken passion, wordless meditation,
Are breathed into it with our respiration
    It is with our life fraught and overfraught.

So that no man there breathes earth's simple breath,
    As if alone on mountains or wide seas;
But nourishes warm life or hastens death
    With joys and sorrows, health and foul disease,
Wisdom and folly, good and evil labours
Incessant of his multitudinous neighbors;
    He in his turn affecting all of these.

That City's atmosphere is dark and dense,
    Although not many exiles wander there,
With many a potent evil influence,
    Each adding poison to the poisoned air
Infections of unutterable sadness
Infections of incalculable madness,
    Infections of incurable despair.

---

* Excerpted from "The City of Dreadful Night," (1874), by the 19th Century British poet James Thomson, better known as "B.V."

They have much wisdom yet they are not wise,
  They have much goodness yet they do not well,
(The fools we know have their own Paradise,
  The wicked also have their proper Hell):
They have much strength but still their doom is stronger,
Much patience but their time endureth longer
  Much valor but life mocks it with some spell.

They are most rational and yet insane:
  An outward madness not to be controlled;
A perfect reason in the central brain,
  Which has no power, but sittest wan and cold.
And sees the madness, and foresees as plainly
The ruin in its path, and trieth vainly
  To cheat itself refusing to be bold.

And some are great in rank and wealth and power,
  And some renowned for genius and for worth;
And some are poor and mean, who brook and cower
  And shrink from notice, and accept all dearth
Of body, heart and soul, and leave to others
All boons of life; yet these and those are brothers,
  The saddest and the weariest men on earth.

Wherever men are gathered, all the air
  Is charged with human feeling, human thought;
Each shout and cry and laugh, each curse and prayer,
  Are into its vibrations surely wrought. . . .

What Do You Think?

1. In your own words, describe the city as Thomson sees it. Is he referring to a real city? What else might he be referring to?

2. Suppose you were asked to respond to Thomson. What would you say?

2. VIEWS OF THE FUTURE

*Some scientists view the problem of pollution with considerable alarm
and forecast grave trouble ahead. The next two articles concern
predictions about the future. Do they seem justified?*

The Poisoned Environment *

*Man is poisoning his air, water, and land. So says Cornell University
scientist Lamont Cole. Might we one day suffer a shortage of these
vital ingredients?*

The United States . . . is burning so much coal, oil, and gas in
its factories, said Dr. Cole, that we are pouring carbon dioxide and other
gasses into our environment faster than the soil and oceans can assimilate
it.

DEPLETION

At the same time, said Dr. Cole, we are paving grassland at a rate
of about one million acres a year, thus removing oxygen from the air
that would have otherwise been put there by the greenery in that one
million acres.

"When and if we reach the point where the rate of combustion
exceeds the rate of photosynthesis," warned Dr. Cole, "the oxygen
content of the atmosphere will actually decrease. Indeed there is evidence that it may already be declining around our largest cities, like
New York and Philadelphia."

If the nitrogen in the air should decline at the same rate as the
oxygen, said Dr. Cole, the effect might be even more disastrous.

"Depending upon which step in the nitrogen cycle on earth broke
down," said Dr. Cole, "the nitrogen might disappear altogether, it might
be replaced by poisonous ammonia, or it might remain with life itself
disappearing for want of a way to use in building proteins."

Man is eroding his land almost as fast as he's polluting his air,
Dr. Cole said.

The establishment of irrigation systems alone has eroded much of
the soil in nine out of ten countries, he said, including most of the
workable land in Asia, the Middle East, and Africa.

---

* Excerpted from "Vision of a Polluted World," December 18, 1967. © 1967
The Los Angeles Times.

ASWAN

"Ever since a dam was built at Aswan in 1902," Dr. Cole said, "the soils of Egypt have been deteriorating through salinization and productivity has decreased. The new Aswan Dam is designed to bring another million acres of land under irrigation, and it may well prove to be the ultimate disaster for Egypt."

Not even the oceans have escaped man's growing tendency to pollute his own environment, Dr. Cole said.

"We are dumping as many as a half million substances into the oceans," he said, "such as pesticides, radioisotopes, and detergents and to which the earth's living forms have never before had to try to adapt." If the tanker Torrey Canyon [1] had carried herbicides instead of oil, Dr. Cole suggested, photosynthesis in the entire North Sea might have stopped.

POPULATION

All this can be avoided, Dr. Cole said, if the earth's people would only stop overpopulating the globe.

"When the British assumed the rule of India two centuries ago, the population was about 60 million," Dr. Cole said.

"Today, it is about 500 million and most of its land problems have been created in the past century through deforestation and plowing and the resulting erosion and siltation, all of which stems from efforts to support this fantastic population growth."

Get Out of Town? *

Air pollution is a major health hazard during much of the year in Los Angeles. Could the same be said of your city?

"Everyone who can do so should move away from the smoggiest parts of Los Angeles, San Bernardino, and Riverside counties," sixty members of the UCLA medical faculty advised yesterday.

Their statement said air pollution is a major health hazard during much of the year and that it is a critical urban problem facing Southern California's metropolitan districts.

The sixty signers also said that as UCLA medical professors and

---

* Excerpted from "Scientists Say Flee Smoggy L. A." *San Francisco Chronicle.* © 1968 *The Los Angeles Times.*

[1] A tanker that ran aground off England, discharging its cargo of oil into the sea and destroying animal life and despoiling beaches.

scientists they have assumed a "collective responsibility" to warn the community of the health hazards of air pollution.

[Some of the views of Dr. William Hildemann, one of the signers, follow.]

The . . . Los Angeles smog problem will not be solved until the automobile industry is forced by law to make cars emit exhaust fumes at much lower levels than now accepted. . . .

[V]oters should make a special point of voting only for candidates or office holders who support adoption and rigid enforcement of strict automobile emission controls and to beware of officials who talk about smog but take no constructive action. . . .

Although some people are optimistic enough to think that Los Angeles' smog problem will be solved in another ten years or so, I'm not sure we can wait that long. . . .

The harmful effects of smog accumulating over another ten years may be physically intolerable. . . .

Recommending that it would be prudent for people to move to avoid respiratory disease may have no more impact than the cancer warnings printed on cigarette packages.

What Do You Think?

1. Dr. Cole seems to think there is one underlying problem with which the world must deal. What is that problem as he sees it? Would you agree or disagree? Explain.
2. Is pollution a problem in your locale? What kinds of pollution are being created? What is local government doing about it?
3. Why are the UCLA doctors so upset? Do you think it is right for them to issue such a statement? Might such a statement frighten the public? Explain.

3. THE CITIES WAR ON SMOG

Los Angeles is often called the center of air pollution in the nation, but this is not true (New York, Chicago, and Philadelphia rank as worse). The next two readings explain in part what Los Angeles and St. Louis are doing to control their air pollution problems. Which approach seems the most effective?

Are Some Auto Controls the Answer? *

What objections might be made to this form of pollution abatement?

Smog now hangs heavy over 26 California counties—about 12,000 square miles of land. University of California smog researchers estimate that more than 50 million pounds of contaminants are daily spewed out into the air just by motor vehicles. And farmers estimate crop damage of more than $100 million a year is due to all types of air pollution.

In many respects, California already leads the nation in air pollution control. But it still has a long way to go to lick this problem.

In curtailing stationary air pollutants, some California counties are making significant headway.

For example, Los Angeles's strict regulations have virtually eliminated the production of smog by home and industry. With stringent checks on open fire, incinerator burning, emissions of organic solvents, and metallurgical processes, the county's Air Pollution Control District says it eliminates more than 5,000 tons of smog a day.

CONTROL CALLED STRICTEST

But pollution control districts at the local level now exist in only 16 of California's 53 counties. A newly formed Air Resources Board will soon pressure other counties to set up their own antismog program. If they don't, the state now is empowered to do it for them.

California's controls over motor vehicle smog contaminants—hydrocarbons and carbon monoxide—are the strictest in the nation. But devices to limit smog producing exhaust fumes are required only on new cars. Eighty per cent of the cars on California's highways—some 8 million—are still unequipped with these controls. And there isn't even a state certified used car exhaust device available now to motorists.

Over 80 per cent of California's 10.5 million registered vehicles now carry smog checking crankcase devices. The law requires their use on all new cars as well as used cars when ownership is changed.

But there is some indication that certain crankcase devices are not doing the job and perhaps even impairing the engine efficiency of some cars. This now is being examined by auto-makers.

EFFECTIVENESS DISPUTED

Despite this, California air pollution officials disagree sharply over the actual effectiveness of auto devices in curtailing smog. And at least

---

* Excerpted from Curtis J. Sitomer, "California Wars on Smog." Reprinted by permission from *The Christian Science Monitor.* © 1967 The Christian Science Publishing Society. All rights reserved.

one local pollution officer questions the standards set up to test their efficiency.

Eric P. Grant, executive officer of California's Air Resources Board, staunchly defends the state's auto control program. He says that the auto industry is meeting present state standards for regulating hydrocarbon emissions and making major headway in checking other smog producing elements. And he is confident that carmakers will meet even more stringent control standards scheduled to take hold in 1970. These are state-set standards. Mr. Grant says that these state auto controls together with effective programs for curbing stationary sources of smog at local levels will ultimately spell victory over air pollution for California.

Robert M. Barsky, Los Angeles deputy air pollution control officer, disagrees. . . .

He says present state requirements are not strict enough to win the war on smog in Los Angeles. Half of the state's cars swarm along the freeways of this southern California megalopolis. And pollution experts estimate that these autos contribute over 90 per cent of the smog which thickly blankets the Los Angeles basin on "red alert" days.

The Los Angeles official also charges that the so-called "averaging" concept used by the state in testing exhaust devices on new cars is faulty. "First of all, the manufacturers choose the cars to be tested," he says. "They're bound to pick the ones whose smog control devices work the best."

"They then use a small sample. And if the average emission of hydrocarbons is no more than 275 parts per million, the whole fleet passes the test."

DETERIORATION CITED

Mr. Barsky says that there is no allowance for wear. "The devices deteriorate and become less effective over a typical 50,000 mile life span of an auto," he explains.

Other critics of the state's program point out that present motor vehicle control devices are designed to reduce only hydrocarbons.

They say another principal ingredient of smog—oxides of nitrogen —may actually be on the rise because of the approach car manufacturers now take to reduce hydrocarbons and carbon monoxide. . . .

The ultimate solution, others say, is to make the electric car the dominant source of transportation in smog bound urban areas. But this movement has gained little support so far. . . .

"Solving the smog problem particularly with regard to the automobile is within the grasp of existing technology," [Mr. Barsky] says.

"Just set standards on new car exhaust controls high enough to do the job. And enact legislation requiring devices on used cars."

The pressure of public opinion can force this issue. It may cost the car buyer a little more in the end. But if we develop the control mechanisms and hang on a price ticket, he'll pay the extra cost," the Los Angeles air pollution officer forecasts.

If Mr. Barsky's reasoning is correct—and few here are likely to take issue with him—it will be the people of California who will have to grit their teeth . . . if they are to stand their ground against smog.

Shall We Fine Drivers? *

Given the limitations of present devices, is it fair to fine drivers whose automobiles lay down smoke screens? This is what one city is attempting to do.

St. Louis drivers are finding that the flashing red light on that police car trailing them doesn't necessarily mean that they have just exceeded the speed limit. They may have violated the city's air pollution ordinance.

Thirty-five specially trained police officers are ticketing drivers whose automobiles and trucks lay down smoke screens. The officers underwent intensive training to help determine when drivers are violating the new law.

The ordinance prohibits the emission of exhaust fumes so dense that 40 per cent of light intensity cannot pass through them. This equates with a reading of 2 on the Ringelmann Chart, a device with shadings from gray to black used to read smoke emission.

The emission of such dense exhaust for more than 10 seconds from a standing automobile or for more than 100 yards from a moving car is a violation subject to a fine of $1 to $500 and 90 days in jail.

First violators generally are being fined $10 and court costs.

At the conclusion of one of the training sessions, an officer raised his hand. "Just one question," he said, directing it to Charles M. Copley, Jr., city Air Pollution Control Commissioner, "will it hold up in court when a lawyer gets up there?"

"One never knows until one tries," Mr. Copley replied.

His deputy commissioner, Paul Mydler, conducted the practical lessons on reading smoke emissions. A calibrated smoke generator producing any density desired was used.

Training amounted to a 24 hour course in the use of Ringelmann and equivalent systems, which enable visual determination of smoke emissions on scales ranging from zero to 100 per cent density.

---

* "St. Louis Puts Pollution Police on Trail of Offending Motorists." Reprinted by permission from *The Christian Science Monitor.* © 1968 The Christian Science Publishing Society. All rights reserved.

Only one of the 11 tickets issued thus far has been contested in court, and the case was continued.

Cpl. Howard J. Biley of the police radar unit noted that "cold weather is making it a little more difficult to read the smoke so we have to be a little more careful."

Patrolman Eugene L. Sieweing of the truck-taxi unit added that steam emitted from automobiles in cold weather also makes reading emissions more difficult.

Publicity given the air pollution enforcement program evidently jogged some trucking firms into making needed corrections, he said.

What Do You Think?

1. Check the list of cities below (1967 ranking, from worst, #1, to best). Where does your area stand on the air pollution scale? Do you consider this to be good or bad? Explain your reasoning.

    1. New York
    2. Chicago
    3. Philadelphia
    4. Los Angeles-Long Beach
    5. Cleveland
    6. Pittsburgh
    7. Boston
    8. Newark
    9. Detroit
    10. St. Louis
    11. Gary-Hammond-East Chicago, Ind.
    12. Akron, Ohio
    13. Baltimore
    14. Indianapolis
    15. Wilmington, Del.
    16. Louisville, Ky.
    17. Jersey City
    18. Washington, D. C.
    19. Cincinnati
    20. Milwaukee
    21. Paterson-Clifton-Passaic, N.J.
    22. Canton, Ohio
    23. Youngstown, Ohio
    24. Toledo, Ohio
    25. Kansas City, Mo.

2. What "ultimate solutions" for the smog program are suggested? Which do you think would be most effective? Why?

3. While the articles do not mention the problem, politics plays a big role in the attempts to control air pollution. What political considerations must be considered? If you were running for office, what would your position be on air pollution control?

4. What do you think of the St. Louis approach? Would it work in your area?

4. THE CONSEQUENCES OF POLLUTION *

The problem of pollution of the environment by insecticides and other chemicals was forcefully brought to the attention of the nation by the writer Rachel Carson. While not, strictly speaking, an urban problem, the consequences of such poisoning are felt by city dwellers. Have you seen what pesticides can do?

There was once a town in the heart of America where all life seemed to live in harmony with its surroundings. The town lay in the midst of a checkerboard of prosperous farms, with fields of grain and hillsides of orchards where, in spring, white clouds of bloom drifted above the green fields. In autumn, oak and maple and birch set up a blaze of color that flamed and flickered across a backdrop of pines. Then foxes barked in the hills and deer silently crossed the fields, half hidden in the mists of the fall mornings.

Along the roads, laurel, viburnum and alder, great ferns and wild flowers delighted the travelers' eye through much of the year. Even in winter the roadsides were places of beauty, where countless birds came to feed on the berries and on the seed heads of the dried weeds rising above the snow. The countryside was, in fact, famous for the abundance and variety of its bird life, and when the flood of migrants was pouring through in spring and fall, people traveled from great distances to observe them. Others came to fish the streams, which flowed clear and cold out of the hills and contained shady pools where trout lay. So it had been from the days many years ago when the first settlers raised their houses, sank their wells and built their barns.

Then a strange blight crept over the area and everything began to change. Some evil spell had settled on the community; mysterious maladies swept the flocks of chickens, the cattle and sheep sickened and died. Everywhere was a shadow of death. The farmers spoke of much illness among their families. In the town the doctors had become more and more puzzled by new kinds of sickness appearing among their patients. There had been several sudden and unexplained deaths, not only among adults but even among children, who would be stricken suddenly while at play and die within a few hours.

There was a strange stillness. The birds, for example—where had they gone? Many people spoke of them, puzzled and disturbed. The feeding stations in the backyards were deserted. The few birds seen

---

* Excerpted from Rachel Carson, *Silent Spring*. Boston, Mass.: Houghton Mifflin Company, 1964.

anywhere were moribund; they trembled violently and could not fly. It was a spring without voices. On the morning that had once throbbed with the dawn chorus of robins, catbirds, doves, jays, wrens, and scores of other bird voices there was now no sound; only silence lay over the fields and woods and marsh.

On the farms the hens brooded, but no chicks hatched. The farmers complained they were unable to raise any pigs—the litters were small and the young survived only a few days. The apple trees were coming into bloom but no bees droned among the blossoms, so there was no pollination and there would be no fruit.

The roadsides, once so attractive, were now lined with browned and withered vegetation as though swept by fire. These, too, were silent, deserted by all living things. Even the streams were now lifeless. Anglers no longer visited them, for all the fish were dead.

In the gutters under the eaves and between the shingles of the roofs, a white granular powder still showed a few patches; some weeks before it had fallen like snow upon the roofs and the lawns, the fields and the streams.

No witchcraft, no enemy action had silenced the rebirth of new life on this stricken world. The people had done it themselves.

This town does not actually exist, but it might easily have a thousand counterparts in America or elsewhere in the world. I know of no community that has experienced all the misfortunes I have described. Yet every one of these disasters has actually happened somewhere, and many real communities have already suffered a substantial number of them. A grim specter has crept upon us almost unnoticed, and this imagined tragedy may easily become a stark reality we all shall know.

The history of life on earth has been a history of interaction between living things and their surroundings. To a large extent, the physical form and the habits of the earth's vegetation and its animal life have been molded by the environment. Considering the whole span of earthly time, the opposite effect, in which life actually modifies its surroundings, has been relatively slight. Only within the moment of time represented by the present century has one species—man—acquired significant power to alter the nature of his world.

During the past quarter century this power has not only increased to one of disturbing magnitude but it has changed in character. The most alarming of all man's assaults upon the environment is the contamination of air, earth, rivers, and sea with dangerous and even lethal materials. This pollution is for the most part irrecoverable; the chain of evil it initiates not only in the world that must support life but in living tissues is for the most part irreversible. In this now universal contamination of the environment, chemicals are the sinister and little-recognized partners of radiation in changing the very nature of the world—the very nature of its life. Strontium 90, released through nuclear explosions into the air, comes to earth in rain or drifts down as fallout, lodges in soil, enters into the grass or corn or wheat grown there, and in time takes up its abode in the bones of a human being, there to remain until his death. Similarly, chemicals sprayed on croplands or forests or gardens live long in soil, entering into living organisms, passing from one to another in a chain of poisoning and death. Or they pass mysteriously by underground streams until they emerge and, through the alchemy of air and sunlight, combine into new forms that kill vegetation, sicken cattle, work unknown harm on those who drink from once-pure wells. As Albert Schweitzer has said, "Man can hardly even recognize the devils of his own creation."

What Do You Think?

1.   What is the nature of the danger seen by the author? Do you regard it as a danger?
2.   Critics of the author have claimed that she overstated her case. Investigate the problem from other sources and see if they can confirm or deny her basic idea.

5. FERTILIZERS AND POLLUTION *

Has it ever occurred to you that the farmer, in fertilizing his land, contributes to water pollution?

Are you massively intruding into your environment?

If you ever fertilize a lawn, garden, or field, the answer is probably yes. "Massive intrusion" is what happens when people do something that changes the chemical balance of nature over a large territory. . . .

Last year 6 million tons of nitrogen fertilizer were used on United States farms. According to Dr. Commoner [a biologist at Washington University in St. Louis] a conservative estimate of 15 per cent of this nitrogen is washed away into rivers and lakes. Another 15 per cent evaporates into the air.

"This means that, annually, about 0.9 million tons of nitrogen reaches surface waters from agricultural sources, where it joins about 0.6 million tons of nitrogen generated by municipal wastes. At the same time approximately 0.9 million tons of nitrogen probably enters the air from

---

* Excerpted from "Fertilizer Linked to Pollution." Reprinted by permission from *The Christian Science Monitor.* © 1968 The Christian Science Publishing Society. All rights reserved.

agricultural sources, annually, where it joins about 2.5 million tons of nitrogen produced by power plants and automobile transport," Dr. Commoner said.

Thus, farm-based pollution may be running in close competition with city-based pollution for the title of "worst offender."

What Do You Think?

1. We need food. We need clean water. Is it possible to resolve this conflict? Consult your biology and chemistry teachers for their view on the problem.
2. The question of pollution is a technical one. Should the people vote on a solution? Why or why not?

6. TEEN-AGERS TAKE PLEA TO CONGRESS *

Some people claim that there is nothing that teen-agers can do about our major problems. A group of young people from Cleveland have proven that the young can have an impact. Is "youth power" a force in your school?

It may have represented a harbinger of a new political force across the continent—the event that was happening in the mammoth hearing room of the Rayburn House Office Building.

Six unusual witnesses gave strong, concise statements to the congressional committee. They presented petitions signed by 13,000 citizens of their city. Then they answered questions without hesitation and with fluency.

The unusualness about these witnesses before the House Committee on Public Works was their age—all were in their teens.

The high school seniors from Cleveland paid their own way here to testify before the committee that is considering new water-quality legislation.

Committee members seemed impressed. It was a form of "youth power" they did not know existed. Rep. John A. Blatnik (D) of Minnesota, committee chairman, said he believed it was the first time in the history of Congress high school students had appeared as witnesses on current legislation.

---

* By Robert Cahn, *The Christian Science Monitor,* March 10, 1969. Reprinted by permission from The Christian Science Monitor. © 1969 The Christian Science Publishing Society. All rights reserved.

DEMANDS OUTLINED

Their petitions, gathered on their own and by fellow teen-agers at the six schools in a week's time, stated their demands:

"We, the undersigned, citizens of the Cleveland area, are concerned over the future of our environment and of Lake Erie in particular. We want prompt and energetic action in this session of Congress to clean up the waters of our nation. What we want from the water-quality act of 1969 with its amendments are:

"A crash attack on the pollution that is killing Lake Erie; enough money to produce results in a hurry; enforcement of statutes already in effect . . ."

BALANCE THREATENED

"We haven't much time; the cumulative effects of our environmental mismanagement are catching up with us," said Jeffrey T. Kline, from Hawken, a private school.

"Is it your right to hand down to us contaminated lakes and rivers that are obviously detrimental to the ecological balance of our environment?" asked Mary Heston, from Laurel School. "Sewage is still dumped into Lake Erie, chemicals are still flushed into it, and it continues to degenerate. Why don't we do something drastic now!"

After noting that for almost 300 years the country has been fighting an enemy either abroad or within the country, Ronald M. Traub of Shaker Heights High School said that the new enemy is water pollution.

EXTRAORDINARY AWARENESS

"Our friends in many other ways are our enemies in this field," Ronald said. "These enemies are big business and local government. Big business, one of the greatest offenders in water pollution, fails to understand . . . that water courses are public property, and those who use and abuse them are accountable to the public and local government. Local government shirks its responsibility when it decides in favor of private profit to the disadvantage of the public."

Ronald had first gotten interested in water pollution in an urban-problems class. Jeffrey got his start while studying at the Cleveland Natural Science Museum. Mary studied oceanography during last summer in a course at the University of Maine and has decided she wants to work on "thermal alteration."

Obviously these high school students were extraordinary in their awareness of the problems of pollution. But they also were normal in that they have discovered they can't swim in Lake Erie any more; it isn't a pretty sight; it gives off bad odors. The lake is dying. And they want something done about it before it is too late.

Virginia Robinson, from Hathaway Brown School, suggested it may be necessary for Congress to re-evaluate priorities. Perhaps pollution should be as important as highway construction, she said, fully aware that the Committee on Public Works also passed out highway funds.

"Gentlemen, there must be no politics in the pollution problem," she said.

What Do You Think?

1. The news story states that the teen-agers paid their own way to Washington for the hearing. They each spent a good deal of money to do this. Would you spend anything to help solve critical problems for the nation? Which problem?

2. Is there a problem in your area about which you could testify to a federal, state, or local agency? If there is such a problem, are you willing to do the research necessary to give adequate testimony? Why or why not?

3. Comment on the following quotation: "Those fool youngsters . . . they ought to stay out in the playgrounds where they belong and let the adults run the country."

7. SCIENTIFIC POSSIBILITIES OFFER HOPE *

Scientists are even now devising new approaches which will cut down on the poisoning of our world. But is there time?

The founders of our cities regarded air and water the way the Indians did buffalo. There was always more where the last supply came from, and nature took away whatever people polluted. Smog and streams no longer safe to wade in have reminded our generation that nature's bounty is not infinite.

The city is a growing component of a global ecological system that we barely have begun to understand. Instruments in orbiting satellites will soon help environmental scientists detect, trace, and predict global trends. Changes may be accelerated at the same time by such projects as the American Water and Power Alliance's proposal to redistribute water throughout the North American continent. Whole cities may seem in a few more decades to have been badly placed.

Until the weather makers perfect their art, or we put cities under

---

* Excerpted from *Science and the City*, U. S. Department of Housing and Urban Development.

some kind of glass, nature will meter the input of air to them and handle the output in its whimsical ways. Yet we no longer need to contaminate the winds that blow through cities with such great volumes of foul gas from our vehicles, factories, and homes as we do now. It is no longer necessary to use fuel that gives off smoke and harmful fumes in densely populated places, or to let city dumps smolder day and night. By using electrical power and modern means of refuse disposal, we could lessen the city's pollution of the earth's atmosphere.

With modern technology we also could reduce the city's contamination of water. It enters and leaves the city through the umbilical cords designed and built by men. Chemical, mechanical, and civil engineers are capable now of improving many of both the input and the output lines in ways that would help the whole country get more use and pleasure from its water resources.

Municipal water and sewage systems, of course, are the responsibility of men intent on minimizing taxes. The demands placed on these systems, on the other hand, are determined by men intent on maximizing profits. Each group has given a little and taken a little from the other —but often has taken a little more than it gave. The result has been increasing extravagance with the earth's water.

TRASH IN THE KITCHENS

American engineers have built completely closed ecological systems for astronauts. They may have to for our grandchildren, too, if we do not amend some of our methods. We still have alternatives, luckily, such as changing our food-handling, temperature-governing and plumbing practices.

Although our refuse, garbage and other solid waste matter already total 800,000,000 pounds a day, we go right on lugging food into our kitchens in bottles and boxes that cannot be compacted or consumed when emptied. Such wrappings are overtaxing the trucks that haul our trash away. Why do we not tax the producers of nonreturnable, nondegradable containers instead of ourselves? They would quickly find substitutes, and we would not have to buy so many garbage trucks.

We heat and cool our homes with machinery we purchase with scarcely any regard for the amount of water they require. We use bathroom and kitchen appliances that send quantities of water down the drain so great they dismay cost conscious chemical engineers. Although utility and other big companies are spending millions to minimize their additions to pollutants in air and water, we are still paying little attention to the efficiency of things in our homes.

The electric garbage grinder under the kitchen sink in many new homes is an intriguing example of a convenience with side effects that the users tend to disregard. Some cities have forbidden its use because of its effects on their disposal systems; others have required its use, and some even have helped to pay for such grinders. Most of us, unfortunately, take the systems that bring and take things from urban homes for granted and pay scant heed to the problems that may be created elsewhere.

A city must be drained to prevent floods, but spring showers could be used to flush the streets in long hot summers if we kept some of the rainwater in rooftop or other reservoirs. When storm and sanitary sewers are combined, the tubing must be large enough to carry great surges—but this is not the only possible way to reduce the danger of overflows of untreated sewage into family basements.

Chicago is considering a $100,000,000 test of an imaginative scheme to store storm water in tunnels 700 feet below the surface, use it to generate electric power, and lift it back to the surface for further use.

Environmental engineers have many ideas. It might be possible, for example, to treat sewage in the big pipes that carry it to discharge points more effectively than nature does after it reaches a river that carries the water to another city downstream. It also might be technically feasible and economically attractive to transport more of the solid matter out of the city in pipelines—and thus reduce the number of trucks disturbing our sleep by banging their way through the streets.

UTILITY TUNNELS

A university campus is a microcosm of a city. There you often find utility tunnels between the buildings. All the pipes and wires needed to serve the occupants of several buildings go through these multi-purpose tunnels. This makes it easier to repair or replace any particular pipe or wire. If we had such tunnels under city streets, traffic would not be held up so often by men with signs saying "dig we must" (such as you see in Manhattan). Might not tunnels reduce our electric, telephone, gas, and other bills?

Alaskans call such big tubes "utilidors." They have made indoor plumbing reliable there, and cost benefit studies might show that they would be good investment in milder climates, too. It might pay, for example, to move some solid matter through vacuum tubing. Do we remove snow from our streets efficiently? Must vehicles in which people ride be delayed so much by men maneuvering and unloading long trucks? Could not many more things flow through pipes than do now?

What Do You Think?

There is a possible danger in relying on science to solve everything. What could that danger be? Do you think it is actually a problem or merely something that might become a problem?

ACTIVITIES FOR INVOLVEMENT

1.   Investigate the efforts being made by your community to control pollution. Arrange an interview with a local official who knows about this problem, and get a list of the priorities established in your area for pollution control.

2.   Send out a survey team to check any areas in your community which may be causing pollution. Prepare a report for the class in which you explain what you believe are the causes of any instances located, and then make a list of suggestions as to how the causes might be eliminated.

3.   Ask someone from the automobile industry to talk about smog control and what is being done in Detroit to remedy this problem.

4.   Call your local medical society and get its view on the health hazards of pollution in your area. If there is a problem, what should you do about it?

5.   Try to write a poem of your own (review Reading 1 in this chapter) about your city, its virtues, and its defects.

6.   Reread Reading 7. Take any one of the ideas suggested in the reading and examine it further. Prepare a brief research paper in which you describe your findings.

7.   Have two members of the class role play one of the following situations:

· Two garbage collectors in New York discussing the food habits of people.

· Two visitors from another planet visiting an American city during an evening traffic jam.

· Two city dwellers in Los Angeles discussing the effects of smog.

· A policeman giving an angry driver a ticket for speeding.

· A farmer arguing against limiting the use of fertilizers.

· Two secretaries complaining about riding to and from work on crowded city buses.

6

What Can
Be Done?

This is an age of planning. Or, more accurately, this is an age when many people talk about planning. It is easy to accept the idea that plans are necessary for orderly development. It is quite another matter to accept planning when these plans differ from your own conception of what is correct or interfere with your property rights or with some other aspect of your life.

Nevertheless, cities today have planning departments associated with the city government; large universities have departments in city and regional planning; and the demand for planners is increasing. As the population of the nation continues to rise and at the same time to concentrate in four or five large areas, there will be still greater concern over the quality of life being led by Americans. It is projected that by the year 2000 over 280 million Americans will be living in urban areas.

Herman Kahn and Anthony J. Wiener, writing in *Daedalus*,[1] identify three areas which they predict will hold roughly one-half of the population of the nation in the year 2000. They call these huge megalopolises "Boswash, Chipitts, and Sansan." Can you identify these areas?

Kahn and Wiener see "Boswash" as providing homes for close to 80 million people on the narrow Atlantic seacoast between Washington, D. C., and Boston. "Chipitts" will include those cities concentrated around the Great Lakes, and "Sansan" will stretch from Santa Barbara (or even San Francisco) to San Diego on the Pacific Coast.

---

[1] The Journal of the American Academy of Arts and Sciences. "Toward the Year 2000: Work in Progress," *Daedalus*, Summer, 1967.

Because of the differing environments and the different types of people who will be attracted to each of these immense population centers, each will develop its own kind of character and living style.

Other predictors also mention the areas of Florida and Texas, where there is currently a population growth comparable to that of the three megalopolises above.

If these predictions are at all accurate, or even if they miss the mark by a considerable margin, it is easy to see why there is so much talk of planning today. There is no question that we have room for a much greater population; we need only look at the population density of Indonesia or England, for example, to see that the United States can hold many millions more people. What we must ask is this: 1. What kind of a nation do we wish to live in in the year 2000? 2. What are we willing to pay for that nation in terms of taxes and restraints on individual freedom?

The planners state that we can deliberately create a nation which will provide the good life for its citizens. We will live in a heavily populated world, but there need be little sense of crowding. There can be plenty of open space and recreational areas. Public transportation facilities can be available to all with little inconvenience or disruption of life. Air and water can be safe for all.

Those opposing planning argue that to implement such plans would require great restrictions on individual freedom. Their main concern is that the planners will eventually be telling everyone what to do and how to do it. This group also argues that the dreams of the planners are just that—dreams for which we cannot afford to pay.

Perhaps most people accept a position between the two extremes. They recognize the need for some kind of orderly growth within the nation and accept the fact that planning may be the tool by which it may be accomplished. At the same time they are wary as to the amount of power given to planners and anxious about the cost of recreating the American environment.

What kinds of things do planners have to think about when they set out to create a city or a city plan? Most of our cities were not planned from the start and just grew for many years before there was a plan created for their growth. Rarely does a planner have the chance to begin from scratch—as was done, for example, in Reston, Virginia; Columbia, Maryland; and Irvine, California. Each of these is designed to be a comprehensive town in which individuals can work and live in comfort. Both Reston and Columbia are close to the nation's capital, and many people commute to Washington. Irvine has as its focal point one of the campuses of the University of California. It is expected that other planned communities will be created in the near future.

However, the planning of America's urban life will deal mainly with established cities and their suburbs. The various commissions, local political pressure groups, state legislatures, and others affected by the problems of urban-suburban living will have to hammer out solutions to the problems we face. On these solutions will hinge the future quality of American life.

The following readings are designed to give some understanding of the problem of planning and to acquaint you with what is presently being done to improve our urban future.

1.   SOME PROBLEMS REVIEWED *

Large-scale migration to cities and attempts at urban renewal are by no means new. Robert C. Weaver, the first person to head the Department of Housing and Urban Development, has written widely about urban renewal. The following excerpt gives some historical background and raises some interesting questions. How would you answer these questions?

Urban renewal, with which our National Government has been experimenting for the past dozen or so years, is an old, old story for the governments of many nations. When London was all but destroyed by fire in 1666, the rebuilding of the city was carried out under acts passed by Parliament and supervised by a board of six commissioners, three of them appointed by the King, and three chosen by the city. It was in every way a major national effort. The rebuilding of Paris by Baron Hassman, a century ago under Napoleon III, was also a national effort, not unrelated to political realities. The wide avenues of that city, which still charm all who view them, were designed in large part to facilitate the movement of troops in the event of civil disturbance.

At the end of World War II, many of the cities of Europe and Asia were left in ruins. Almost two decades have flown by since then, and today the gaunt devastation has been swept away and magnificent new cities have arisen like a phoenix from the ashes. In nearly every case this, too, was accomplished with the guidance and assistance of national governments.

Urban development has been an issue of national policy in most

* Excerpted from *The Urban Complex,* by Robert C. Weaver. Copyright 1955, 1959, by Atlanta University; Copyright 1960 by the Academy of Political Science; Copyright 1964 by Wayne State University; Copyright 1960, 1961, 1964, by Robert C. Weaver. Used by permission of Doubleday & Co., Inc.

countries for a long time. What impresses us today is the fantastic acceleration of national activity in this field. Urbanization is not new. The things that are being done to cope with it are not new. The means by which these things are being done are not very new, either. What IS new is the great momentum which has developed behind this movement of urbanization —a momentum which has been building up for centuries, and shows every sign of continuing to build, and build, and build in the decades ahead.

There is also another basic consideration which must be kept in mind. It is the fact that in most instances urban renewal has involved a major change in cost of housing. Slum clearance and rebuilding by private enterprise on the land made available through urban renewal usually produced much higher-priced housing. Thus, urban renewal generated two major problems: it created the need for relocation housing for those families which were initially displaced, and it involved permanent displacement of a large class of families formerly living in the areas affected by the new program.

From the beginning of the urban renewal program relocation has been a major issue. Problems of large dimensions developed in cities like Chicago, Detroit, and New York, where low income families were either forced out by economic and political pressures, required to purchase second-hand properties at inflated prices, or were further overcrowded in contiguous areas already substandard or in the process of becoming substandard due, primarily, to overoccupancy. With the exception of those families which qualified for the available public housing (in which they had priority), the relocation experience could be, and was often, unfortunate and fraught with extreme hardships for many of those involved.

Occasionally areas subjected to renewal were occupied either by families which had created socially viable, if physically blighted, neighborhoods, or by a large number of homeowners or both. Clearly, relocation of those who had been long identified with an area, who were attached to their neighborhood, and who had long utilized its institutions, created real psychological problems. For homeowners, both psychological and economic problems were involved. The former are obvious—the threat to security incident to displacement from a home that was owned by a family. The second was more complex—loss of real or imputed value incident to leaving an area which had sentimental and imputed great economic worth. This, too, was complicated by the difficulty of acquiring, in a tight housing market, a comparable dwelling with the equity derived from the old house.

At the same time, priority for displaced families in public housing projects, when combined with concentration of urban renewal areas on sites inhabited largely by nonwhites, increased the proportion of colored tenants in subsidized projects. As a consequence, many racially integrated public housing projects in the North became predominantly or exclusively Negro developments largely as a result of the pressure created by the displacement incident to urban renewal.

In Washington, D. C., for example, where relocation was carried out with care and adequate records were maintained reflecting where families moved, some of the older residential areas were adversely affected. Southwest Washington was cleared only at the price of creating the need for additional clearance in parts of Northwest Washington and the spread of blight in a segment of the Northeast.

Between 1940 and 1950, over 7,000,000 people moved to the suburbs of this nation. More than 2,000,000 whites deserted central cities at the same time that some 1,300,000 nonwhites moved in. These figures, when they became available in the mid-1950's, gave rise to much speculation and apprehension about the future of the American cities. Public officials, housing specialists, and journalists asked: Are the large cities in this nation about to become nonwhite ghettos? Will the metropolitan areas of tomorrow have a core of low-income, colored families surrounded by middle- and upper-income whites in the suburbs? Does this mean Negro political domination in the larger urban communities? Will downtown businesses and cultural institutions wither away from lack of support?

Large-scale migration to cities is no recent phenomenon. In this country many nationality and ethnic groups have been involved, and each of these has at first gravitated to areas contiguous to downtown business. Every new group has been resented on the basis of imputed inferior status. Negroes, Puerto Ricans, and Mexicans are the most recent components in this process.

Middle- and upper-income families have been moving to the suburbs for decades, and the majority of the core areas suffered rather sizable out-migration during the depression and in the prosperous 1940's. Thus, for more than a quarter of a century, central cities have attracted fewer newcomers than their suburbs. Such growth as they experience was due to the excess of births over deaths rather than to net in-migration.

Basically, therefore, the situation in the 1950's was a projection of trends which have been with us for some time. It did, however have two peculiarities. It took place at a time when the exodus from the central city to the suburbs was at a peak, and a large number of the newcomers to the larger metropolitan areas belonged to readily identified minority groups. Both of these circumstances led to a considerable amount of distortion. Some have confused coincidence with causation. To them the desertion of the central city by middle- and upper-income whites was purely and simply a means of escape from Negroes. Others seem to feel that large scale movement of low-income families to industrial centers was peculiar to the migration of nonwhites and that perpetual, enforced residential segregation was an inevitable consequence of such population movement.

Actually, this was not a new type of migration. Rather widespread enforced racial residential segregation had given a unique cast to a recurring phenomenon. Because metropolitan areas do not afford the most recent migrants free movement and equal opportunities for housing, their concentration in the core areas of many urban communities creates perplexing problems. What we do about the color line in shelter will determine whether these problems become chronic or dissolve into solutions which have typified earlier migrations to these same industrial cities.

Suburbanization through migration has been almost a universal phenomenon in the United States and a fairly general one in Canada during the last quarter of a century. Actually it is more than a phenomenon of the American hemisphere. Copenhagen, too, evidenced this development. There, as in this Nation, higher-income families are seeking shelter in the suburbs while low-income groups are finding shelter in the central city. A recent study of these movements concludes that "the central city may become increasingly the domicile of those whose income, type of work and marital status makes residence in the more expensive and more family centered suburban areas economically impossible or socially undesirable."

Here we have an instance of a European metropolis, with practically no nonwhite population, where migration is producing an increasingly (economically) homogeneous population in the central city, composed increasingly of low-income persons.

Many metropolitan areas in the United States where suburbanization of this type has occurred have extremely small nonwhite populations. Binghamton, New York; Brockton, Massachusetts; Cedar Rapids, Iowa; Duluth, Minnesota; Superior, Wisconsin; and Fall River-New Bedford, Massachusetts are just a few examples. Thus color alone cannot account for the migration of over seven million people to the nation's suburbs in the 1940–1950 decade.

Until fifty years ago, the Negro remained, for the most part, outside the process of urbanization. He was primarily an American peasant— perhaps the only basically peasant component in the Nation. In the last fifty years, however, he has joined the march to the cities and has caught up with and surpassed even the white rate of urbanization.

Negroes have become mobile, but their mobility is still very different from that of other Americans; it, too, is a search for a better life, but it is still a search more confined and more subject to disaster and tragedy and uncertainty than other Americans find. Urbanization has set the stage for a new and better life for Negroes, and over a third have realized this in economic terms. But the development of a really viable life pattern in the cities remains largely unfinished business for the majority of Negro Americans.

By 1960, 69.8 per cent of the United States population was urban; among Negroes, 72.4 per cent were urban. But even these figures under-estimate the urbanization of Negroes, for while the vast majoriy of urban Negroes live in central cities, about a quarter of urban whites live in suburban areas. The movement out of the South, to the Northern and Western cities, has been steady from 1910 when 87 per cent of the non-whites lived in the South, to today, when slightly over half live in the South. Even in the latter region the majority of Negroes now live in cities.

The basic cause of the northward migration was undoubtedly eco-nomic. Great waves of Negro migration have been stimulated by periods of economic growth, particularly the expansion of assembly line produc-tion during each of the two world wars and the decades immediately thereafter. Northern industries actually solicited the migration of Negroes during World War I. But even without solicitation, it has been the search for full-time employment and higher wages that brought the Negro migrant to the city from the Southern farm. Within the South, too, it is the search for jobs that has urbanized the Negro population.

It is a revealing experience to dip back into the literature of the early industrial revolution, when rural migrants were crowding the cities. They lived under conditions and with results very similar to those we find today. William Blake was not referring to our Harlems and our ghettos when he wrote:

> I wander thro' each charter'd street
> Near where the charter'd Thames does flow,
> And mark in every face I meet
> Marks of weakness, marks of woe.

Hogarth and Dickens painted a picture of urban misery and poverty, of social disorganization and disease, which was greater than anything we have to face today. And in this country, from the 1840's on, Euro-pean immigrants were crowded into our cities and the same frightful toll was taken in the disruption of families, in illegitimacy, in the desertion by husbands, in disease and alcoholism and madness. We need only read the descriptions of the urban ghettos by Jacob Riis and his contemporaries to discover that some of our problems are not new. They are more shocking and dangerous, however, because they occur and continue at a time when ours is an affluent society.

When finally Negroes began to move out of the social backwash of the South and into the Northern cities, they became the latest in the sequence of people to undergo urban misery. One indicator of the social disorganization incident to urbanization is the incidence of family disorganization. But this is not a recent or racial phenomenon; it is one of the most predictable consequences of rapid urbanization under crowded and impoverished circumstances.

Everything we see today in crowded Negro urban settlements was noted by social workers in the crowded immigrant quarter of our cities at the turn of the century—whether these were Jewish, Italian, Polish, or what have you. There was overcrowding; unrelated people living in the same households; poverty and discouragement; and the observable consequences. And we can go further back to seventeenth-century England. The rate of illegitimacy then was so disturbing that Sir William Petty, one of the fathers of political economy, proposed a system of government maternity hospitals for pregnant unmarried women, and urged that the illegitimate children born in them become wards of the state.

Today, the strains upon the nonwhite family continue to be aggravated by overcrowding. Thus, in the metropolitan areas in 1960, 28.5 per cent of the nonwhite households in rental units lived under crowded circumstances, compared to only 14 per cent of the whites. It is particularly significant that even at the income level of $6000 to $7000 the crowding remains just as high, and the disadvantage, compared to white households, as great.

If family stability is judged by the presence of both husband and wife, it declines with migration and increases with rising income. Among Southern rural nonwhites, for example, there is considerably more stability than in Northern cities at every income level. And in both South and North, the stable nonwhite families become more numerous as income rises.

In the Northeastern and Midwestern cities, very high percentages of households with female heads occur among the poor nonwhites. Thus, if households with incomes under $3000 and whose heads are in the 35 to 44 year age bracket are considered, 1960 census data reveal that over 50 per cent have female heads; for families with incomes between $3000 and $4000, the percentage drops, but is still over 20 per cent; for families with incomes between $4000 and $5000 the percentage drops further, to between 10 and 15 per cent.

Among Southern rural nonwhites, in the poorest families with incomes under $3000, the percentage of families with female heads is only 20 per cent; and it falls in higher brackets to about 5 per cent. Thus, it may be said that in Northern cities there is, by one measure, approximately two and a half times as much instability among nonwhite families as in Southern rural areas; and among the poorest families there is about four or five times as much instability as there is among those better off.

The 1960 census figures for the District of Columbia (a locale often cited as the prototype of Negro crime and family disorganization), offer convincing proof that as the Negro acquires education and becomes integrated into the economic life of our cities, family life becomes more stabilized. Indeed, after Negro families achieved a relatively moderate income, $3000 to $5000 a year, the degree of family stability among Negroes in the District was as high as among whites, using our measure of proportion of husband-wife families.

The history of most ethnic minorities in urban centers of the North and West has been one of initial rejection, gradual acculturation, and eventual absorption. Peoples with different customs and values who were exposed to the process of Americanization modified their beliefs and behavior and thereby achieved a new position in society. Starting, for the most part, as low-income workers, they have been able, in large numbers, to acquire education, obtain better jobs, and achieve higher social status. They have moved out of the slums of yesterday into the suburbs and middle-class neighborhoods of today. This nation offered them middle-class status when and if they evidenced adherence to the dominant culture. For them, there were and are real, tangible, and demonstrable rewards for industry, conformity, and ambition.

Similar rewards are far less general for nonwhite. Thus, the degree of social and economic mobility among this group is less. This circumstance, in turn, is used as justification for perpetuation of second-class status for colored citizens. Yet the fact of the matter is that the immigrant was criticized because of differences in culture, behavior, and appearance which he could and often did change. The nonwhite, even when he had modified cultural and behavioral patterns, is stuck with pigmentation which in our society is a badge of difference and inferiority.

Before the complex nature of the situation occasions despair and hopelessness, let us view briefly the other side of the changes in our society which have brought about these more intricate problems. Concern for slum clearance, effectuating a solid economic base for our central cities, and arresting the spread of blight have created new, if reluctant, allies in meeting these problems. Increasingly, it is apparent that slum clearance, rehabilitation, and urban renewal must come to grips with the human problems involved. Either we increase appreciably the social, economic, and residential mobility of nonwhites and other ethnic minorities, or we will continue to tear down one slum only to create others and spread blight. Programs in this field are threatened by large elements in the society relegated to a perpetual submerged status.

Cities seriously concerned with urban renewal are being made to appreciate that, both in terms of human potential and dollars and cents, there are sound grounds for public programs designed to accelerate the participation of those who are now rejected from the mainstream of modern urban life. Herein lies another significant change in intergroup relations. For generations, many Americans have been troubled by the constitutional issues inherent in racial discrimination. Gunnar Myrdal identified the color problem in this Nation as a moral issue. The color bar has made race relations a crucial international concern. Current events are adding a new dimension. Now it is becoming apparent that there are significant economic and political reasons for action to accelerate the effective participation of the latest newcomers in urban life. No doubt, we will have to do much experimentation in this area, but once there is a commitment to meet the issue, productive techniques can and will be developed.

What Do You Think?

1. What, according to Dr. Weaver, was unusual about the migration to the cities during the Fifties? Venture some suggestions as to what could have been done at that time to have prevented or limited our present crisis.
2. Some scholars have written of the breakup in Negro family life brought about by the move to the cities. What does Weaver have to say about this? Do you agree or disagree with him? Explain.
3. Why do so many Negroes live in the central cities? Why are so few in the suburbs? How do you feel about this situation?

2.   WHAT BECAME OF THE GOOD OLD DAYS? *

Harrison Salisbury seems to confirm some of the statements made by Weaver. Yet there is something in this reading that calls for a return to the past. Would this be possible?

The projects are political deserts. The precinct bosses have been wiped out with the slum. They do not seem to come back. No one cares whether the new residents vote or not. There is no basket at Thanksgiving. No boss to fix it up when Jerry gets into trouble with the police. The residents have no organization of their own and are discouraged from having any.

"We don't want none of them organizers in here," one manager of a project told me. "All they do is stir up trouble. Used to be some organizers around here. But we cleared them out good. Lotsa Communists. That's what they were."

---

* Excerpted from *The Shook Up Generation,* by Harrison Salisbury, New York, N. Y.: Harper & Row, 1958. Copyright 1958 by Harrison Salisbury.

Lack of political and social organization was not characteristic of low-rent projects when they first started going up in the late 1930's. Housing specialists understood that if you simply built barracks for the poor you were only creating a new ghetto. In the early days the housing projects had good social components.

Long before the old slum was torn down social service teams went in to prepare the people for what lay ahead. They arranged to give displaced persons priority in the new buildings. Care was taken to provide social facilities to replace those torn out. Community centers, child care centers, playgrounds and other facilities were built. (But never as many as were needed because of shortage of money.) It was recognized that families of low cultural background would have to be helped to adjust or they might turn their new surroundings into a replica of the old.

One simple and effective device used in the early days was the "rent girl." The young woman was, in fact, a social service worker or student. Each month she went from door to door and collected the rent. She stopped in for a cup of coffee or tea. She knew all the women. She knew their troubles. She was regarded as a friend—not an inquisitive social worker. She was able to help new families get started and stop trouble before it became serious. She could tell the manager what his tenants were up to. It was an effective device. It was cheap. It was simple.

But bureaucratization set in, economy waves, reduction of everything to the lowest possible denominator. It was always easy to cut the social services. They weren't essential. They were the "frills" seized on by real estate interests, stupid congressmen, sensation mongering tabloid newspapers. The "rent girls" quickly vanished. Now, the tenant is required to come to the manager's office to pay his rent. The relationship is strictly impersonal. No one steps foot in the apartment until after the trouble starts. No one has any way of learning what is happening to the people. No one really cares.

In the early days the projects had tenants' associations. They were lively affairs, full of politics, sprouting with good works, enthusiasm, and argument. They were training grounds in democracy. Then the Communists moved in on them. Soon the associations were devoting more time to the party line than to the lives of the people.

Now they have been destroyed, root and branch. Most of them found their way into the Attorney General's subversive list. They were harassed and harried out of existence.

But the destruction of the associations created a vacuum. We threw the baby out with the bath water. The big low-cost projects have no organizations, no political interests. Their community structure has been turned into social mush by stupidity and bureaucracy.

There is a "Tenants Guild" at one project which epitomizes the level to which organization has sunk. Mrs. George Washington Astor is the leader of this guild. She told me about her work, dropping her 250 pound bulk into a plush armchair and sighing heavily.

The project has a population of more than fifteen thousand. There are eighteen members of the guild.

What Do You Think?

1. Can you suggest a way to enrich the dreary life of the public housing projects? Explain.
2. What does Salisbury mean by bureaucracy? Is this good or bad? Why do we have bureaucracies?

3. WHAT ABOUT A MODEL CITY?

The Model Cities legislation [1] provides for a comprehensive attack on social, economic, and physical problems in blighted areas. Under its terms, federal, state, and local public and private efforts give assistance to cities to plan and carry out imaginative proposals for "model" neighborhoods. If you were mayor, what new ideas would you suggest for your city?

The Generation Gap in Antislum Programs *

Poor people wish to exercise control over their own destinies. The following reading describes this attitude.

Less than five minutes drive from the center of St. Louis, 33 drab, boxlike buildings poke into the sky. Each is 11 stories high. Each is alike—a slab of concrete, 11 vertical rows of windows across each side. Many of the windows are smashed.

This is Pruitt-Igoe. Within these 33 buildings live some 10,000 people—all Negroes. Pruitt-Igoe is a public housing project. When it was built with local and federal money in 1954, architects and public officials hailed it as a major break-through in housing for the poor.

Today Pruitt-Igoe is an eyesore and a breeding ground for crime and disease. Sociologist Lee Rainwater, in a recent issue of *The Public Interest,* a quarterly journal, wrote: "The words 'Pruitt-Igoe' have become a household term . . . for the worst in ghetto living . . . No other public

---

[1] Cities and Metropolitan Development Act, passed by Congress in 1966.

* Excerpted from Norman Lunger, "Model Cities: A Voice for the Poor." Reprinted from *Senior Scholastic,* © 1968 by Scholastic Magazines, Inc.

housing project in the country approaches it in terms of vacancies (more than 20 per cent), tenant concerns and anxieties, physical deterioration."

Almost everyone now says that building Pruitt-Igoe was a mistake. Cramming people into massive housing projects without solving other problems created a slum just about as bad as the one Pruitt-Igoe replaced.

Pruitt-Igoe belongs to the "first generation" of U. S. antislum measures. Officials at all levels of government hope to avoid such mistakes in the "second generation" presently under way.

One of the most significant of these second generation programs is the federal Model Cities program. Unlike most antislum measures in the past, the Model Cities program aims to do many things at once—in contrast to past antislum measures which usually focused on only one thing at a time. (One project aimed to clear away decaying housing, another aimed to build new housing, still another aimed to improve health services in the slums.)

Under the Model Cities program, Congress has voted a first-year appropriation of $311 million to coordinate various separate projects. Most of the money for the projects themselves will still come from other federal, state, and local programs. . . .

Government officials are aware that many of the poor look with distrust on antislum programs. The officials are seeking to combat this by forming advisory boards and including on these boards representatives of the "target areas," the areas that will be affected. A federal government brochure on the Model Cities Program declares: "Planning must be carried out with as well as for people living in the affected areas." Federal officials repeatedly list "citizen participation" as a key ingredient of the Model Cities program.

Is "citizen participation" a good idea? Opinions are varied. An official in Rochester told me he supported the idea, but then noted that it involved problems as well as advantages. "There are almost as many groups claiming to represent the poor as there are individual poor people," he said. "We invite these groups to nominate members to our antipoverty council. FIGHT has been asked to choose a representative. But FIGHT only represents part of the poor community, and we also have to take into account the wishes of other groups. Sometimes it's hard to strike the right balance.

In St. Louis, a young man at the Pruitt-Igoe housing project scoffed at the suggestion that "citizen participation" would be meaningful. "Sure they tell you they've got representatives of the poor," he remarked. "But look who they've got—preachers, black businessmen, Uncle Toms. Those guys don't speak for the cats in the street." . . .

At a time of rising tensions in the slums, few government officials at any level are eager to see still more militancy. That's why they hope that "citizen participation" can give poor people a meaningful role in planning changes in their own communities. Poor people who become actively involved in such a role, the officials argue, will take a more responsible view of the problems involved and be less likely to make "exorbitant" demands.

It may work, or it may not work, officials admit. But at least it should help avoid any future mistakes such as Pruitt-Igoe.

What Do You Think?

1. What are some of the reasons people criticize the building of the Pruitt-Igoe project? If you had to plan for public housing, how would you do it? What considerations would influence your decisions? Explain.

2. There is a lot of talk about participation by the poor in the planning and running of programs designed to help them. How do you feel about this matter?

ACTIVITIES FOR INVOLVEMENT

1. Choose a chairman and a committee to unify the various reports the class or committees have made as previous activities. Write a summary statement identifying what the class believes to be of highest priority in your city, or the city nearest you. The final plan should be submitted to the entire class for ratification and amendment. Once the entire process is completed, copies should be given to the local planning commission, at a meeting of that commission.

2. After the final report is adopted prepare a debate on the following question: Resolved: That city planning commissions be given the power to put their plans into effect without approval by the local law-making body.

3. Now that most of the work on this unit has been completed, begin a campaign to get students included as advisory members to local commissions and boards. See the mayor and other officials and get their endorsement. Make a list of all those whom you must contact and who can exert influence for what you want.

4. In small groups discuss the future of your city and other cities in the United States. Keep no notes and make the atmosphere informal. Which of your city's problems concern you? What can you, as an individual, do about these problems? What are you going to do?

BIBLIOGRAPHY
For Further Study

Books

ABRAMS, CHARLES · *The City Is The Frontier* · New York, N. Y.: Harper Colophon Books, 1965.

BLUMENFELD, HANS · *The Modern Metropolis* · Cambridge, Mass.: MIT Press, 1967.

BROWN, CLAUDE · *Manchild in the Promised Land* · New York, N. Y.: Signet Books, 1966. (paperback)

CARSON, RACHEL · *Silent Spring* · Boston, Mass.: Houghton Mifflin, 1962.

CLARK, KENNETH · *Dark Ghetto* · New York, N. Y.: Harper & Row, 1965.

CONOT, ROBERT · *Rivers of Blood, Years of Darkness* · New York, N. Y.: Bantam Books, 1967. (paperback)

DRAKE, ST. CLAIR, HORACE R. GAYTON · *Black Metropolis* · (Vols I & II) New York, N. Y.: Harper Torchbooks, 1945. (paperback)

Editors of Scientific American · *Cities* · New York, N. Y.: Alfred A. Knopf, 1965.

GORDON, RICHARD E., GORDON, KATHERINE, MAX GUNTHER · *The Split Level Trap* · New York, N. Y.: Dell Publishing Co., 1967. (paperback)

GORDON, MITCHELL · *Sick Cities* · Baltimore, Md.: Penguin Books, 1945. (paperback)

HANDLIN, OSCAR · *The Uprooted* · New York, N. Y.: Grosset and Dunlap, 1951.

HARRINGTON, MICHAEL · *The Other America: Poverty in the United States* · Baltimore, Md.: Penguin Books, 1963. (paperback)

HOOVER, EDGAR A., RAYMOND VERNON · *Anatomy of a Metropolis* · Garden City, N. Y.: Doubleday Anchor 1962. (paperback)

JACOBS, JANE · *The Death and Life of Great American Cities* · New York, N. Y:. Vintage, 1961. (paperback)

KEATS, JOHN · *The Insolent Chariots* · Philadelphia, Pa.: Lippincott, 1958.

LAURENTS, ARTHUR · *West Side Story* · New York, N. Y.: Random House, 1957.

LOWE, JEANNE · *Cities in a Race With Time: Progress and Poverty in America's Renewing Cities* · New York, N. Y.: Vintage, 1968. (paperback)

MILLER, WARREN · *The Cool World* · Greenwich, Conn.: Fawcett World Library, 1964.

MOYNIHAN, DANIEL PATRICK, NATHAN GLAZER · *Beyond The Melting Pot* · Cambridge, Mass.: MIT Press, 1963.

MUMFORD, LEWIS · *The City in History* · New York, N. Y.: Harcourt, Brace & World, 1961.

MUMFORD, LEWIS · *The Highway and the City* · New York, N. Y.: The New American Library, 1962.

SILBERMAN, CHARLES E. · *Crisis in Black and White* · New York, N. Y.: Random House, 1964.

SPECTORSKY, A. C. · *The Exurbanites* · Philadelphia, Pa.: Lippincott, 1955.

STEFFENS, LINCOLN · *The Shame of the Cities* · New York, N. Y.: Hill and Wang, 1957.

THOMAS, PIRI · *Down These Mean Streets* · New York, N. Y.: Alfred A. Knopf, 1967.

VERNON, RAYMOND · *Metropolis 1985* · New York, N. Y.: Doubleday Anchor, 1965. (paperback)

WEAVER, ROBERT C. · *The Urban Complex* · New York, N. Y.: Doubleday Anchor, 1966.

WRIGHT, NATHAN JR. · *Black Power and Urban Unrest* · New York, N. Y.: Hawthorn Books, Inc., 1967.

Special Reports

The Exploding Metropolis · The Editors of Fortune, Doubleday Anchor, 1958.

Report of the National Advisory Commission on Civil Disorders · (The Kerner Report), 1968.

A Time to Listen . . . A Time To Act · Report of the U. S. Commission on Civil Rights, 1967.

"The U. S. City," *Life,* December 24, 1965.

"The Negro and the Cities," *Life,* March 8, 1968.

"Our Sick Cities," *Look,* September 21, 1965.

"The City," *Psychology Today,* August 1968.

"The Future Metropolis," *Daedalus,* Winter 1961.

"Toward the Year 2000: Work in Progress," *Daedalus,* Summer 1967.

Films

The Problem with Water Is People (30 min; color and B/W; prod. NBC News; dist. McGraw-Hill Films) · Examines the potential crisis in the nation's most vital natural resource—water.

Cities of the Future (25 min; color; CBS News for the "21st Century" Series; dist. McGraw-Hill Films) · Focuses on the creative planning now in progress to surmount current problems. Covers 12 cities around the globe.

A Trip from Chicago (25 min; color; prod. CBS News for the "21st Century" Series; dist. McGraw-Hill Films) · Investigates the means by which people and goods will be transported in the near future. Covers air, land, and sea craft—some operative, some in the design stages.

The City and Its Region (28 min; B/W; 1963; prod. Natl. Film Board of Canada; dist. Sterling Educational Films) · Examines how balance and harmony between city and countryside can be maintained or restored in today's metropolitan regions.

The City and the Future (28 min; B/W; 1963; prod. Natl. Film Board of Canada; dist. Sterling Educational Films) · Explains that cities must choose between low-grade urban sprawl or a new kind of regional city.

The City as Man's Home (28 min; B/W; 1963; prod. Natl. Film Board of Canada; dist. Sterling Educational Films) · Examines how slums, public housing, suburbs, luxury apts. developed. Suggests ways to improve the quality of city life.

The City (11 min; color; 1958; prod. Encyclopaedia Britannica Films) · Scenes of a complex city, including many types of buildings, neighborhoods, transportation facilities, suburban areas, and city government.

The City—Cars or People (28 min; B/W; 1963; prod. Natl. Film Board of Canada; dist. Sterling Educational Films) · Studies the problem of how to make the city accessible without allowing transportation to make it congested and uninhabitable. Shows problems and solutions of several cities.

The City—Heaven and Hell (28 min; B/W; 1963; prod. Natl. Film Board of Canada; dist. Sterling Educational Films) · Outlines the creative and destructive natures of the city in history. Covers elements that caused the creation of the first cities and forces that now threaten the city.

The Changing City (12 min; color; prod. Churchill Films) · Deals with the effects on people of metropolitan living. The use of land and the renewal of old cities are discussed with special reference to the historical pattern of city growth.

Chicago—Midland Metropolis (22 min; color; 1963; prod. Encyclopaedia Britannica Films) · Why Chicago grew and became one of the great cities of the world. Discusses geography, immigration, and industrialization. Notes the changing demands of urban life.

The Uprooted Nation (22 min; color; 1965; prod. Churchill Films) · A close look at the long-term immigration patterns within the United States and their effect on individuals and communities. Utilizes the insights of city planners and demographers, among others.